JOAN OF ARC

JOAN OF ARC

A PLAY IN FIVE ACTS

by

CHARLES DESNOYER

Translated and Adapted by Frank J. Morlock

THE BORGO PRESS

An Imprint of Wildside Press LLC

MMIX

CONTENTS

Cast of Characters 7

Act I, Scene 1: The Vision 9

Act II, Scene 2: The King and the Clown 41

Act II, Scene 3: The Deliverance of Orléans 59

Act II, Scene 4: The Bastion of Tournelles 71

Act III, Scene 5: The Consecration at Rheims 82

Act IV, Scene 6: Compeigne or Treason 105

Act IV, Scene 7: The Judgment 117

Act V, Scene 8: The Prison of Rouen 129

Act V, Scene 9: The Stake 142

Act V, Scene 10: Apotheosis 152

About the Author 155

DEDICATION

To

My daughter Michelle

CAST OF CHARACTERS

KING CHARLES VII
SAINTRAILLES
DUNOIS
LE SIRE DE FLAVY
MARCILLAC
AGNES SOREL
TURLUPIN, the King's fool
WILLIAM TALBOT, son of the Commanding General of
   the English Army
CAPTAIN BAUDRICOURT, Commander of Vaucouleurs
D'ESTIVET, Doctor of the University
THE ARCHANGEL
JACQUES D'ARC
ISABELLE, his wife
LOUISE, his daughter
MARGUERITE, his daughter
JEANNE, his daughter
DURAND LASPART, a young peasant
TYNDAL SACK ET MORT, Leader of the English Free-
   booters
ROBERT, a freebooter

WILLIAM, a freebooter
A MESSENGER
An INHABITANT OF ORLÉANS
AN OLD MAN
A WOMAN
A CHILD OF ELEVEN
AN ENGLISH SOLDIER
A RUFFIAN
A HERALD AT ARMS
AN INHABITANT OF RHEIMS
AN ENGLISH OFFICER
A BEADLE
THE GOD OF ARTS
LORDS AND LADIES OF THE COURT OF CHARLES VII, PEASANTS, ENGLISH AND
FRENCH SOLDIERS, PENITENTS, FREEBOOTERS, THE EXECUTIONER
PAGES

ACT I

Scene 1: The Vision

The stage represents the main room of the house of the farmer Jacques d'Arc. To the right, a high chimney with sides jutting out. Also on the right, a door giving on the courtyard. To the left, three doors leading to the interior. Large benches, a big armchair, a table.

AT RISE, in the center of the stage, Jeanne is busy with needlework; near her, Isabelle spins with a wheel; to the right, by the chimney, Jacques grinds a stick which he intends to make into an axe handle. From time to time, he tries to adjust the iron; at the table, Marguerite winnows grain, and Louise puts it in a basket.

LOUISE: (as she puts the grain in the basket) Father, you can boast of having some famous seeds; I am winnowing them like a real cherubim, and my sister Marguerite extracts them as if they were grains of gold.

JACQUES: She's right. It's our gold. Farmers like us

with good seeds. Besides, she's working for you.

LOUISE: How's that, father?

JACQUES: All that this grain produces will be your dowry with Raimond.

LOUISE: In that case, extract even better, Marguerite. And as for me, I am going to throw my grain higher since I am winnowing for my marriage.

ISABELLE: Right! As for you, Louise, you are not hiding your joy.

LOUISE: My marriage! No, mother! I am neither like Jeannette, who doesn't know there are men on earth; nor like Marguerite, who sighs deeply.

MARGUERITE: Louise!

LOUISE: Eh! Don't blush! Do like me. I say everything out loud: Raimond pleases me, Raimond suits me, and the more children I have, the better I'll be.

JEANNE: (bringing her work to her mother) Is this all right, mother?

ISABELLE: (examining it) Very nice, very nice. (calling her husband) Look Jacques, the beautiful shirts your daughter Jeannette has made you.

JACQUES: (coming closer and looking) Ah, indeed. I bet that Captain de Vaucouleurs, the Lord de Baudricourt, doesn't have any as pretty. (hugging Joan) Thanks, my little Jeannette.

(Joan sits back down and begins to sew. Jacques returns to his tools.)

LOUISE: Say, father. Without being too curious, in which field are you going to sow my dowry?

JACQUES: In the plot to the left as you leave Domremy.

LOUISE: Do the plot to the right instead, and I will bring ten sacks more to my husband.

JACQUES: The plot to the right, near the Chenu woods?

LOUISE: Yes.

JACQUES: You're forgetting that the tree of the fairies is on that side?

LOUISE: The tree of the ladies.

JACQUES: Ladies or fairies, it's all one. The shadow of that tree on your wheat can bring you bad luck.

LOUISE: Ah, bah! They say an evil spirit can do nothing against a young girl. After I'm married, I don't say.

JEANNE: But father, a really long time ago, many years, the Curé of Domremy blessed the tree of the ladies.

JACQUES: All the same, in the days when you didn't go there so often, you were more gay.

LOUISE: The tree had nothing to do with it, father. And I was laughing under all the leaves.

ISABELLE: Say, Jacques. Now look how the day's getting on and nephew Durand Lapart hasn't arrived today.

LOUISE: Mother, now Marguerite is blushing again.

MARGUERITE: You mock everybody.

ISABELLE: No, my daughter. Louise isn't making fun, just laughing; but Louise, like us, desires your marriage with your cousin Durand Lapart. His mother is my sister. She's always been good to us all. Three months ago, Jeannette even spent two weeks with her at little Burcy and at Vaucouleurs. Durand is good; devoted to his family.

LOUISE: Yes, Cousin Durand isn't very brave. But he's a brave lad.

MARGUERITE: Louise, he cannot lack courage, having gone as far as the Loire, accompanying the provisions that his father sold.

LOUISE: Only, I see that when he returned he took the longer way.

JACQUES: My word, that's excusable. Do you know that between the marshes of Lorraine, where we are, and Orléans, there are troops who don't observe the truce they have over there?

LOUISE: Yes, the troops of the English adventurer Tyndal.

JACQUES: Say his name in full. Because of his pillagings and murders they call him more than ever, Tyndal, Sack and Kill.

(Joan listens with interest. Isabelle points out Joan's look to her husband.)

ISABELLE: (low) Jacques, be careful.

JACQUES: (low, looking at Isabelle) That's just. (aloud) Come, let's speak no more of that. Times have changed. Night's going to come soon. I'm going to go see how work is coming in the filed. Marguerite, go to the pasture field and have them return the animals. We are going to have a storm.

MARGUERITE: (rising) Yes, father.

JEANNE: Mother, before the bad weather, do you want me to go see little Simonne Musmer who is ill?

ISABELLE: Go, my daughter. I know that this poor child, like all those who are sick in the village, is happier when it's you caring for them.

JACQUES: (low to his wife) Jeannette is going to pass once more before the beech tree of The Ladies. She always says a prayer there.

ISABELLE: There's an image of Our Lady there.

JACQUES: It seems to me that thereabouts there's an evil spirit who provides visions.

ISABELLE: I am going to accompany her.

JACQUES: That's the thing.

ISABELLE: (aloud) Jeannette, I'm going to bring some provisions for the patient.

JEANNE: You are really good, mother.

JACQUES: (as he is about to leave with Marguerite by the right; to Jeannette and his wife) Come on; each on his way. Louise, straighten up everything and think about supper.

LOUISE: Everything will be ready when you return. (the others all leave) Come, let's put everything in order. (she hums and she straightens things up) My mother's spinning wheel, Jeannette's work. And my winnow basket, and my dowry. (stopping before the grain Marguerite was winnowing) Gentlemen grain. Try to each become an ear of corn; very thick, very rich. And they will grind you and put you in beautiful linen sacks. And they will exchange you against all the Parisian pounds I will give to Raimond. (singing as she continues) A woman will ruin France; a virgin will save her.

DURAND: (entering by the back) Hello, cousin.

LOUISE: Heavens! At last, Cousin Durand Lapart.

DURAND: Where is everybody?

LOUISE: (getting excited) Now there's a little of everybody.

DURAND: Everybody well? My uncle? my aunt?

LOUISE: And Marguerite, too.

DURAND: Ah! and Jeannette?

LOUISE: Jeannette is always a little in the clouds. But I really know she was afraid for you; she didn't say anything but she will be very delighted to see you again.

DURAND: Ah, yes. And Jeannette?

LOUISE: My word! She comes and goes. It doesn't seem to be a big thing for her.

DURAND: (excitedly) Isn't she the best and the wisest girl in the village?

LOUISE: Oh! one moment. To speak well of her, I would shout louder than you. As for those ideas, she's a bit— Except for when one speaks of war, of Tyndal, Sack and Kill, of the King, of France, in the end she appears not to hear. She almost always is dreaming and seems to speak to God. As for the rest, the poor daughters of Jacques d'Arc are no more than all the others. As for me, I dream of Raimond, whose wife I am going to become. Marguerite thinks of an ingrate who went across the Loire—

DURAND: And Jeannette?

LOUISE: My word! If Jeannette thinks, it's never of you. And if you insist on knowing, (pointing to Joan who enters) she will tell you so herself. (to Joan) Here, Jeannette. Here's Durand.

JEANNE: (entering) Hello, Cousin Durand.

DURAND: Hello, Jeannette.

LOUISE: (to Joan) Here. While I go get supper ready, tell him that since it's agreed within the family that he will marry Marguerite, it's not right for him not to love her more. 'Bye, cousin. (mimicking him) And Jeannette? Well, here she is, Jeannette. Talk to her now.

JEANNE: (who's taken up her work) Is it true, what she said, Durand? That you don't love, Marguerite?

DURAND: Oh—no. Quite certainly—Marguerite.

JEANNE: She is good, sweet. And she'll make you happy.

DURAND: You think so?

JEANNE: Yes, because she loves you a lot.

DURAND: Ah! And you Jeanne. Don't you love anyone?

JEANNE: Me?

DURAND: Yes, you.

JEANNE: Yes!

DURAND: A lot?

JEANNE: A lot.

DURAND: Who do you love?

JEANNE: France!

DURAND: (sadly) Poor Jeannette. Still her ideas.

JACQUES: (in the doorway) Hey! Wife! Hey! Marguerite, come on. Durand's got here. (entering) At last, here you are, my boy. (Isabelle and Marguerite follow him)

DURAND: Hello, uncle. Hello, aunt. Hello, Marguerite.

MARGUERITE: Hello, cousin.

ISABELLE: Do you know, it's more than a month since you left?

DURAND: Listen, things don't go as one would like. And what must be especially avoided are the big highways.

JACQUES: Things are really still bad?

DURAND: Worse than ever. It's the beginning of the end.

LOUISE: (bringing a tureen of soup) To table! Here's the soup!

JACQUES: That's it. When rain falls one receives a traveler. And the best thing to do is to go to dinner.

LOUISE: (indicating the places) Father in the middle in his big armchair. Then me, then mother, then Jeannette. On the other side, Marguerite and Durand. (low to Marguerite) Huh? Am I sweet?

JACQUES: (ready to sit) Come on. You mustn't be less hungry than we are.

JEANNE: (stopping him sweetly) Father—

JACQUES: That's just. The prayer. Speak it, my daughter.

JEANNE: (standing as do all the others) Lord, let the power of Christ bless us and the food we are going to take. And may France be saved.

JACQUES: (low to Durand as everyone sits) She has to mix France a bit into everything.

ISABELLE: Well, let's see, Durand. What did you see on your trip? What did you hear?

DURAND: What I heard most were curses against Queen Isabelle.

JACQUES: The wife of the late King Charles, the Foolish?

LOUISE: The Mother of the Dauphin, Charles VII?

DURAND: Well, it's a famous concert about her. Instead of caring for her husband, said one, she let him suffer from cold and hunger in a tower of the Louvre. She spent all the money in the treasury, said another. She sold her daughter in a marriage to the King of England, said a third. And now that her son-in-law is dead she wants France to belong to the son of her daughter, a little Englishman of seven. (Joan listens with growing emotion) And to achieve that, she's kicking out her son, Charles VII, and making war on him. And she's set the Duke of Burgundy on the English side. And because of all this they pillage us, burn us out, kill us. And then they all cursed her.

JACQUES: Let's curse her, too

ISABELLE: The debauched woman!

LOUISE: The evil mother!

DURAND: The thief of the treasury!

JACQUES: The merchant of our blood. (all rise except Joan)

ALL: Let's curse her! Curse her!

LOUISE: (sitting back with the others, then singing) A woman has ruined France—

DURAND: And the other couplet—

LOUISE: (singing) A virgin will save her.

(Joan rises excitedly)

JACQUES: What do you intend to do, Jeannette?

JEANNE: (letting herself fall back) Nothing, father, nothing.

LOUISE: And didn't that make you want to take up arms like our brothers, Durand?

DURAND: No, I am not for war. I don't love the foreigners, but endure what I cannot prevent. As to all these miseries, folks like us; we can do nothing.

JEANNE: (reproachfully; looking at him) Nothing.

(Knocking at the door. The thunder rumbles.)

JACQUES: Open, Louise. It's not good to stay outside in that storm.

LOUISE: (opening the door to D'Estivet and Talbot)

D'ESTIVET: Brave people. Will you allow us to remain a few moments in this house?

JACQUES: All night, if you wish, my father. And in this weather it's the best thing for you to do.

D'ESTIVET: (to Talbot) Milord, I told you the peasant hereabouts is good and hospitable. (to Jacques) Since you permit it, we will await a horseman here, who is to meet us on our way, and who has doubtless been delayed by the bad weather.

DURAND: Wouldn't that be a man of arms—of fifty

years?

D'ESTIVET: You've seen him?

DURAND: No, stay, my father. I am going to tell him that you are waiting for him here. Uncle, with your new guests, you won't have a place for me tonight. I am going to go sleep at the house of Simonne. And tomorrow, at daybreak, I will come say goodbye to you.

JACQUES: That's the thing, my boy.

ISABELLE: I am going to get everything ready. Our son's room is fine for one, but it will have to take two at least.

JEANNE: Mine, mother. I am going to work. If I am tired, I will go join Louise.

TALBOT: I regret so much—

ISABELLE: We do this all the time. Even for the poor who come and ask for asylum.

(Joan passes timidly before Talbot and stops with a sensation of fright before D'Estivet.)

JACQUES: Excuse, gentlemen. She's so timid that sight of you is enough to trouble her. (Joan goes to rejoin her mother)

TALBOT: She's really beautiful. How old?

JACQUES: Seventeen and a half—

TALBOT: You will soon marry her.

JACQUES: (lowering his voice) Don't mention that.

TALBOT: Why's that?

JACQUES: Her distaste for marriage has already earned us a lawsuit.

TALBOT: A law suit?

JACQUES: Yes, a lad from the village, named Tiphaine was completely taken with her two years ago and presumed to take her to court on a promise of marriage he pretended Jeanne made him.

TALBOT: Well?

JACQUES: Well, Milord— She, who is so timid, pleaded her case before the Bailiff at Vaucouleurs and she won. Tiphaine was convicted of lying.

TALBOT: And what did he do then?

JACQUES: My word, for a while he worried me. He's a bold, willful lad, not afraid of anyone. Living with an old mother who alone had an empire over him. But two months later, he disappeared.

TALBOT: What! Disappeared!

JACQUES: During one night, when Domremy was attacked by the English Freebooters, supported by my son and some neighbors, I retreated towards the chateau, and we were able to get there after having defended ourselves against fanatics who fell on us on the way. When we returned a week later to Domremy, Mother Tiphaine was alone. As her son had disappeared, Jeannette took care of her. And the poor woman died in her arms two days later.

TALBOT: And no one ever learned what became of him?

JACQUES: There were indeed, some who said he had joined the enemies. Some pretend to have recognized him, even among the English bandits who attacked us in our marshes. His intent, they are certain, was to profit by the disorder and carry off our daughter. Bully that he was, he always loved his mother deeply and that thought always stopped him. I think, rather, he was carried off by the pillagers and killed in the neighboring woods.

D'ESTIVET: Ah, see, here's Sire de Baudricourt.

JEANNE: (stopping) The Sire de Baudricourt!

BAUDRICOURT: (entering and removing his cape) Gentlemen, it's better here than under the porch of the church.

JACQUES: (pointing to some provisions that Louise has placed on the table) Milords, on this table are things that will refresh you a little. When the rooms are ready, they'll come tell you.

BAUDRICOURT: Thanks, my brave man. Your name?

JACQUES: Jacques d'Arc.

BAUDRICOURT: D'Arc! I've already heard that name.

ISABELLE: (calling Joan, who's stopped everything on hearing the name de Baudricourt) Come on Jeannette!

(Joan follows her father and mother into the interior. Louise and Marguerite are already inside.)

BAUDRICOURT: Well! I'm here, sir. What do you want with me? And what imperious motive made you ask so eagerly for an interview?

D'ESTIVET: Captain, this young cavalier, is the son of Milord Talbot, generalissimo of the English Army.

BAUDRICOURT: Talbot! One of our most formidable enemies.

TALBOT: I've just delivered a message from the Duke of

Burgundy; and passing through Lorraine, I wanted to try to establish a truce here.

BAUDRICOURT: Which is not always observed by your Freebooters.

TALBOT: You know, all France is being subdued under the flag of England.

BAUDRICOURT: You are forgetting that Orléans is valiantly withstanding a siege against your troops; my brother is there with Dunois.

TALBOT: Orléans is reduced to such extremities that it has offered to surrender.

BAUDRICOURT: To the English Regent? To the Duke of Bedford?

TALBOT: Not, rather to the Duke of Burgundy.

BAUDRICOURT: At least he's not a foreigner.

TALBOT: But the Duke of Bedford cannot consent to it. I've been charged by him to go tell the Duke of Burgundy that he didn't beat the thickets for someone else to get the bird.

BAUDRICOURT: So Orléans—

D'ESTIVET: Must surrender in no more than a week.

BAUDRICOURT: And my brother—

D'ESTIVET: He will come himself to tell you the news.

BAUDRICOURT: But King Charles the VII?

D'ESTIVET: Rather, say the pretended Dauphin. King, he is not; he hasn't been blessed.

BAUDRICOURT: You are French, father?

D'ESTIVET: Rallied to our new sovereign and Rector of the University. As soon as the whole realm shall have recognized its true, its only master, Henry of Lancaster.

BAUDRICOURT: Well, while waiting, let the English leave for England.

TALBOT: Sire de Baudricourt, I didn't come to propose an act of cowardice or treason. Charles, who the whole world abandons and who is abandoning himself, appears resigned to the title, King of Bourges. For it is close to that town that his reduced estates are found. Why do you persist obstinately in a war without possible results? Unite yourself to us and let the two nations catch their breath.

BAUDRICOURT: Lord Talbot, I believe in the sincerity of your words, and in the truth of the picture that you are painting me of the condition of France. But don't be astonished if it costs a faithful subject, a French heart—

JACQUES: (returning with Joan and Isabelle) The gentlemen's rooms are ready.

TALBOT: I don't insist, Sire de Baudricourt. We will see each other again in the morning.

BAUDRICOURT: Perhaps night will bring counsel.

TALBOT: Our worthy host. Would you wake us at break of day? We are only going to toss ourselves on our beds.

JACQUES: Don't worry, Milords. You will be awakened early.

(Baudricourt, Talbot and D'Estivet go into the first two rooms to the left. Jacques escorts them to the door.)

ISABELLE: (to Joan) You are going to work here still, Jeannette?

JEANNE: Yes, mother. When I get tired, I will go join Louise.

JACQUES: (having returned) Not too late, my child.

JEANNE: Goodnight, father; goodnight, mother. (They both embrace her and retire. She becomes pensive; she sits in her father's armchair; she takes up her work and starts to sew.) Let's struggle with work against these ideas which already come to assail me. Why is Sire de

Baudricourt here? Why did Duran recount the country's misfortunes before me? I want to remain here, and I feel they are calling me down there. I cannot endure it. The days are weighing me down. Voices speak to me. I don't want to hear them. Ah! work isn't protecting me against them. Weariness from these inner struggles overwhelms me. My God, give me the rest of sleep. (falling asleep little by little) Leave! Leave! I don't want to. I don't want to, (She sleeps. Clouds descend on the stage. A sweet elevated music can be heard. One can distinguish most particularly a motif destined to announce that Joan hears divine voices. The Clouds part.) I can still hear voices. Terror seizes all my members. I am burning. I am shivering. It's a holy fever. (A brilliant cloud opens, revealing the archangel Michael) The Archangel! The holy Archangel!

ARCHANGEL: Jeanne—

JEANNE: He's speaking to me. He's calling me.

ARCHANGEL: Jeanne, go help the King of France.

JEANNE: Oh—I cannot. I don't dare.

ARCHANGEL: Speak to Sire de Baudricourt. He will take you to the King.

JEANNE: The King will reject me.

ARCHANGEL: The King will have a sign to believe you.

JEANNE: I am only a poor girl.

ARCHANGEL: You will raise the siege of Orléans. And you will restore the kingdom to the King.

JEANNE: But to abandon my mother!

ARCHANGEL: Obey! (he begins to vanish)

JEANNE: My brothers from paradise, don't leave me.

ARCHANGEL: Obey.

JEANNE: My brothers from paradise—take me with you. (She collapses exhausted. The clouds dissipate. The original décor reappears. The light is extinguished. Day begins to break through the windows. Jacques enters, followed by Isabelle, and raps softly on the doors of the guests' rooms.)

TALBOT: (from within) Thanks, our host. We are ready.

(Isabelle opens the blinds and the transept at the back. She notices Durand.)

ISABELLE: (through the window) You here already, Durand?

DURAND: (entering from the left) Yes, I am coming to say goodbye to you because I intend to return to little Burcy.

(These three remain at the back as Baudricourt, Talbot and D'Estivet come forward from the left.)

TALBOT: Well, Sire de Baudricourt? Have you decided? Rally to the Duke of Burgundy. The cause you are supporting is desperate.

BAUDRICOURT: I am tempted to believe you and yet—

D'ESTIVET: Yes, you are waiting for a miracle to come to the help of the King of Bourges. Yes, a miracle. For, at this moment, and for some time already, the Kingdom belongs to Henry of England.

JEANNE: (who's been watching them) It belongs to Charles of France.

(Jacques, Isabelle, and Durand rush forward excitedly.)

BAUDRICOURT: Who is this young girl?

JACQUES: Don't pay attention, Milords. (low to Joan) Jeannette—be careful.

TALBOT: (looking at her) The young girl who was so timid last night.

D'ESTIVET: Sire de Baudricourt, she is perhaps your miracle beginning.

BAUDRICOURT: I don't think so. For it seems to me I

recognize her.

JACQUES: You know my daughter?

JEANNE: Yes, Milord: it was I, who escorted by my uncle Lappart to Vaucouleurs; it was I that you rejected, telling me to return to my father to be spanked.

JACQUES: And what did you go without my knowledge to ask of Sire de Baudricourt?

JEANNE: To be taken to the King.

ISABELLE: Jeannette, I beg you, my child—

TALBOT: What noble self confidence!

JACQUES: Jeannette, it's us. Look at us.

D'ESTIVET: This poor girl is going mad.

JEANNE: No. I am not going crazy, but divine voices have told me the pity there is for the kingdom of France. You say simply: The English and the Burgundians are conquerors; but you don't say the men are killed, the women are fleeing into the woods with their children; that the wolves are taking possession of the country. That outside the towns, from Picardy to Germany, there's not a house standing; that famine has come after the war; plague after famine. And that there are towns where the grass is choking the roads, except in the ruts choking with the tumbrels of the dead.

BAUDRICOURT: But here, for the last three years, we are calm.

JEANNE: Calm! Yes, there's no assault and pillage every day. But it's the expectation of evil, it's the tocsin, it's awakening with a start, it's the somber red of arson in the distant heavens. It's war, it's war in the end—this reign of Hell. Where all men die in a condition of mortal sin! God sees it! God wants France to be saved! Sire de Baudricourt—lead me to the Dauphin.

BAUDRICOURT: Who are you?

JEANNE: I come on behalf of the Lord—to whom all France belongs.

BAUDRICOURT: Who is this lord?

JEANNE: The Lord of Heaven, who wishes to give France to the protection of the Dauphin Charles; and it is necessary that I soon appear before him. For no one in the world, neither King, nor Duke, nor King's daughter, nor anyone else can raise up the Kingdom of France again. The only help for it is in me.

TALBOT: What holy enthusiasm!

D'ESTIVET: (aside) She could be a dangerous lunatic.

BAUDRICOURT: And what will you tell the Dauphin?

JEANNE: I will tell him to give me men and weapons, and with them I will deliver Orléans and I will invest the King at Rheims. It is for that I am born.

JACQUES: (with severity) Jeanne, enough! My daughter with soldiers! Before letting her leave like a lost child, I will tell her brothers to drown her in the Meuse, and if they don't, I'll do it myself.

ISABELLE: Jacques!

JEANNE: Father, pardon me, for I honor you and love you, but I must obey my voices.

JACQUES: (enraged) You shall not leave!

JEANNE: (firmly) Father, I will go!

ISABELLE: My poor child! You in the midst of battles! Why, you cannot see even a child die.

JEANNE: It's because of that, mother: the sight of French blood makes my hair stand on end.

ISABELLE: Abandon your mother!

JEANNE: Don't weep, mother; for you are right. My work is not there, and I would prefer to remain sewing near you. But I must go and must do it, since the Lord wills it.

ISABELLE: Jeanne, I beg you—

JACQUES: I order you—

BAUDRICOURT: All this is unnecessary: while waiting for peace there is a truce.

JEANNE: Peace between France and the enemy who has his foot on her throat! That's a lie. Truce! Why this very night, at two leagues from here, didn't they pillage and kill?

D'ESTIVET: You see quite well she's raving.

LOUISE: (rushing in) Father, can we dispose the rooms of our guests?

JACQUES: Why?

LOUISE: Domremy is filled with poor folk who fled last night from the village of Volthern. Tyndal, Sack and Kill ravaged it completely.

DURAND: Jeanne said it.

LOUISE: Jeanne cannot know it; I just saw a refugee who was ahead of all the others.

TALBOT: That's strange.

BAUDRICOURT: Never mind; Jeanne, your devotion is useless. Orléans surrendered about a week ago.

JEANNE: (pointing to D'Estivet) He's the man who told you that, and that man lied.

BAUDRICOURT: I am expecting my brother who was at Orléans with Dunois.

JEANNE: Your brother won't come; and Dunois has sworn not to surrender Orléans.

BAUDRICOURT: And why won't my brother come?

JEANNE: Three days ago he attacked the Fort of Tournelles commanded by Glacidas—and he was slain.

BAUDRICOURT: (moved) My brother!

D'ESTIVET: Eh, what! Such an imposture.

PEASANTS: (entering from the back, followed by a messenger) This way, this way.

MESSENGER: A message for Sire de Baudricourt.

BAUDRICOURT: What am I to learn? (to Messenger) Where are you coming from?

MESSENGER: From Orléans.

BAUDRICOURT: Who sent you?

MESSENGER: Count Dunois, who delivered this letter to me. (Baudricourt takes the letter and opens it. General silence.)

TALBOT: Well?

BAUDRICOURT: (with sorrow and stupefaction) My brother is dead!

DURAND: (in the back, to the people) Jeanne just announced it.

TALBOT: I stand confounded. (to Messenger) Has Orléans surrendered at discretion?

MESSENGER: No, Milord. The besieged have regained courage.

TALBOT: Who revived them?

MESSENGER: The expectation of divine help.

TALBOT: What do you mean?

MESSENGER: They are repeating the prophecy throughout the town.

TALBOT: What prophecy?

MESSENGER: The prediction that a girl from the marshes of Lorraine will deliver Orléans. (stupefied silence broken by Jacques)

JACQUES: No. Even though everything conspires against my will; I won't suffer it.

DURAND: Stop uncle. I am neither captain nor Burgundian, nor Armagnace. I am people. And I feel all that the people feel. Jeanne has made me understand the wrongs of my brothers of the people. It's cowardly to remain locked in at home when brothers cry out to you. Jeanne has given me heart and I am ready to obey her. To follow her everywhere she will go. To defend her, to fight, to get myself killed. Speak, Jeanne. Does God want war?

JEANNE: He wants deliverance.

DURAND: Deliverance. Until death, Jeanne, here's my place.

BAUDRICOURT: But the countryside which separates us from the King is covered with enemies.

JEANNE: God will make my way.

BAUDRICOURT: But if God wants to save us he has no need of soldiers for that.

JEANNE: The soldiers will battle; God will give them

victory.

D'ESTIVET: And God has charged a woman with—

JEANNE: When the strong are losing courage, God stirs up women and children.

DURAND: Jeanne is right. Let her go! God wills it.

PEOPLE: Yes, yes, Let her go.

DURAND: All the money I have. There it is, to buy her a horse.

ALL: (giving money) And me! and me! Here, take. For Jeanne, for Jeanne.

TALBOT: Despite myself I admire her and tremble for our cause.

JEANNE: (kneeling before her father who remains confounded) Father, pardon me.

JACQUES: (recoiling) Be quiet; I am afraid.

ISABELLE: Afraid!

JACQUES: Sorcery.

D'ESTIVET: Sorcery! I'll remember that word.

JEANNE: Mother, mother! Prevent him from cursing me.

ISABELLE: Ah, my God protect me and return my child to me.

LOUISE: Jeanne. Our good Jeanne. Where are you going?

JEANNE: Where my brothers from paradise have told me to go (She starts forward. The peasants make way for her, bowing. Her terrified father remains in his large armchair. Isabelle and Joan's sisters weep, extending their arms to Joan who moves away.)

CURTAIN

ACT II

Scene 2: The King and the Clown

A room in the palace. Everything is prepared for a great feast; the hall is brilliantly lit. Charles is seated. Saintrailles is standing before him.

CHARLES: No, no, my dear Saintrailles, I cannot receive the envoys today. You know quite well my guests are expecting me.

SAINTRAILLES: But, Milord, they are the deputies from Orléans coming to tell you of their hard extremities.

CHARLES: Exactly. And I have no response to give them.

SAINTRAILLES: As for me, Milord, when they recount their miseries to me, and the famine of their fellow citizens, I would not like to be obliged to answer them that the King is dining.

CHARLES: (severely) Saintrailles! (then more softly) Well, look. Cannot you give them some money for supplies?

SAINTRAILLES: Renault de Bouligny, your treasurer, all of whose money is yours, has only four shillings about him.

CHARLES: We must put together some troops and send them some help.

SAINTRAILLES: Troops? And who, Milord, will take arms? Orléans is your last bastion and it's going to fall. The misfortunes are so great that all bend their necks. The doctors of the Church, terrified by our ills, to explain the wrath of God can only repeat: God only afflicts those he loves.

CHARLES: (rising to go) Let's submit to the judgment of Heaven.

SAINTRAILLES: (standing in his way) Yes, sire, and let's receive the help it sends us as well.

CHARLES: Ah! You are going to speak to me again of that young girl?

SAINTRAILLES: For the last three days she's been at Chinon and asks to be presented to you.

CHARLES: But she's a lunatic and Flavy, Marcillac, Pierre de Nauges and the others, just now, were joking about her in a thousand ways. I was laughing with all my heart.

SAINTRAILLES: (presenting his sword) Then, sire, take back this sword.

CHARLES: Your sword!

SAINTRAILLES: I took it up to strike foreigners with its iron. Not to beat against the legs of a useless courtier in its scabbard, or a parasite of your feasts.

CHARLES: You want me to have no friend left at the last day?

SAINTRAILLES: Before that last day comes, I want you to have tested all means, tried every effort; I want to see you fall only when the last muscle of your body will have deserted your courage.

CHARLES: Come, since you insist, I will see this village girl.

SAINTRAILLES: This very day.

CHARLES: No. Get still more information.

SAINTRAILLES: A man is here ready to answer all my questions.

CHARLES: Question him; and if you still believe—. But, you must put it off. In the presence of all these lords, less convinced and more cheerful than you, my poor Saintrailles.

SAINTRAILLES: Fear nothing.

CHARLES: Do you remember that pretended, inspired woman? Wasn't she called Marie of Avignon? When she was in my presence, she was content to tell me that France had much left to suffer and that the angels had presented weapons to her.

SAINTRAILLES: Which, she added, were not for her but for a young girl who would deliver France.

CHARLES: And you imagine that this young girl is the one who—

SAINTRAILLES: I imagine only that no other country on earth is in more need of divine pity than France.

CHARLES: (as he goes) Come for a moment; come join with our friends; you will see what wild joy animates them. It was Sire de Flavy who arranged this feast.

SAINTRAILLES: Yes, the feast of Saturnalia. It's not thus—

CHARLES: Indeed, Saturnalia. All ranks are confounded, turned upside down. The masters have become slaves, and the servants, in turn taking on sumptuous clothes, are being served by their masters with full license to speak the truth. It's Turlupin, my jester, who is going to play the King of France.

SAINTRAILLES: And in his turn, the King of France—

CHARLES: — Is going to wear the fool's cap in place of Turlupin. What do you want? Are not folly and intoxication our only resources against the calamities which weigh on our heads? Come, come then. You will tell me what you think of my feast.

SAINTRAILLES: Sire, I think that no one could lose a kingdom more gaily.

CHARLES: If it must be lost, of all ways, this is the best. (going out)

SAINTRAILLES: (to a page) Let that man enter.

DURAND: (entering; blinded by the light) Ah, how beautiful it is. Why, it hurts the eyes. I've never seen such beautiful churches.

SAINTRAILLES: (who is seated) Approach.

DURAND: Ah! My God! Some one. A man all in gold.

SAINTRAILLES: Approach then.

DURAND: Ah! Milord, Sire. His Majesty, the King.

SAINTRAILLES: I am the Count of Saintrailles.

DURAND: Ah, pardon. I didn't wish to offend you. We are, Jeanne and I, poor peasants from Lorraine, who have never seen—

SAINTRAILLES: Don't be afraid. And answer me—

DURAND: Yes, Milord.

SAINTRAILLES: With whom did you come to Chinon?

DURAND: I came with Jeanne. With two gentlemen; with a messenger of the King; with an archer, with the gentlemen's servants, and—with me.

SAINTRAILLES: What road did you take?

DURAND: Excuse me, we didn't take a road. But because of all the detours we had to take in Burgundian country, we marched 150 leagues.

SAINTRAILLES: And how much time—?

DURAND: Eleven days, without offending you.

SAINTRAILLES: You met with obstacles, doubtless—

DURAND: Ah! Damn! Not to displease you, first of all

we met four big rivers. The Marne, the Aube, the Seine and the Yonne. With that, we didn't stay in the towns; it was necessary to cross all these at the fords and at the end of winter, when waters are high and cold,—saving your respect, it's not easy.

SAINTRAILLES: And where did you stop?

DURAND: In the Abbeys—when we encountered them. If not, I don't know if it is permitted to say it, on the ground.

SAINTRAILLES: Jeanne in the midst of you?

DURAND: Yes, Milord.... In the clothes of a man and wrapped in her traveling cloak.

SAINTRAILLES: All those who accompany her are really devoted to her?

DURAND: Alas, my God, no. The first days, there were those who, as if enraged by the perils she exposed them to, and I heard half of them call her mad and even sorceress. Two of them proposed to put her in some good jail. Others remarked, and these caused me even greater apprehension, that she was young and beautiful.

SAINTRAILLES: Well? Then what?

DURAND: Well, then. Reverence speaking, they saw such great goodness in her that it was as if there was a barrier around her.

SAINTRAILLES: A barrier—

DURAND: A barrier of respect and religion.

SAINTRAILLES: And since then, she's been at Chateau Chinon?

DURAND: She asks, without commanding you, to see the King who refuses to see her. The townsfolk, councilors of the King, came and they declared, as they left her, that she is a creature of God. Ladies, nurses, bourgeois came as well, and she spoke to them so sweetly, so graciously that it made them weep. Oh, Milord, try to get her to speak to the King. As for me, I wouldn't dare, but I believe she will dare. And since she demands it, it must indeed be so, for Jeanne, for France, for me; I, who am only a worm in the ground. But now I'll get myself killed for France and for Jeanne. I beg you Milord, get her to speak to the King. (he falls to his knees)

SAINTRAILLES: Rise, my brave lad. Your prayer will be fulfilled. Bring Jeanne here without losing a moment and let her hold herself in readiness to appear.

DURAND: (enchanted) Ah, thanks. Pardon, excuse! Thanks, Milord. Jeanne is going to be happy. See how happy I am. I rush. I will return. (kissing the hem of Saintrailles' cloak) Thanks again. (rushing out)

SAINTRAILLES: I still hope. Charles is endeavoring to deceive himself. Factitious joy that clings to delirium, laughter full of tears and rage reveal the abasement to which the King is reduced, a generous heart still and what an energetic voice will arise from so much degradation. (looking) Ah, there they all are. Madame Agnes, Flavy, Marcillac. My place is no longer here. I will allow the clowns and courtesans to rejoice. (Goes out a side door. Lords and ladies, crowded around Agnes Sorel, enter noisily.)

AGNES: (to Flavy who gives her his hand) Honor to you, Milord Count, who devised and ordered this feast.

FLAVY: Ought you not to be the Queen of it?

AGNES: And then, wasn't this a way to please the sweet Dauphin whose love is all mine? But wait, see—your intentions haven't been faithfully carried out. (new entry of lords and ladies)

FLAVY: Yes, these indeed are the Saturnalias I dreamed of. Turlupin has come to sit on the throne! They are going to place a royal cloak on his shoulders. (Turlupin, a crown on his head, a sword at his side comes to take his seat on the throne in the midst of applause and bursts of laughter. Pages cover him with a royal cloak.)

FLAVY: (laughing) Long live Turlupin the first!

TURLUPIN: Silence, ladies and gentlemen, or beware

my wrath. I am King; King Charles VII. From now until tomorrow morning. And he has a mission of making me laugh, my court and me. Here he comes now.

(Enter Charles in the costume of the King's jester. He holds a fool's cap in his hands)

CHARLES: Yes. Here he is. Room for the King's fool. He's in spirit today. To each of you a blow with his cap. To each of you a beautiful and good truth. I intend to make you laugh at your own expense.

FLAVY: (laughing) Ah! Ah! We are all disposed to do that, my master.

TURLUPIN: And we order you to do it. Such is our good pleasure.

CHARLES: Well, at you, first of all, Guillaume de Flavy. You be the first to hear me. And to recoil before your image. Or laugh at it, if you dare.

FLAVY: Why not?

CHARLES: We shall see. You are incredulous, Milord de Flavy and when the brave Labire (pointing to him), so terrible on a battlefield, trembles and crosses himself when he hears thunder growl, you raise your face, bursting out laughing. "There's nothing to frighten me, to dominate me," you say, "neither high nor low, nor under my feet nor above my head." Poor lunatic! The most foolish of us all. The most worthy to bear the fool's cap. You have your gods, too. Your gods to whom you sacrifice blindly: luxury, envy, pride. All the vices of Hell. To them, and through them, you are devouring your patrimony. Now, you are devouring the leavings of royalty, and if you could, you would devour France.

FLAVY: (enraged) Milord!

CHARLES: (laughing) Ah, ah, ah. You're getting angry; you're getting carried away—against a poor clown. I was quite sure you wouldn't laugh until the end.

MARCILLAC: Bravo! bravo! Long live Turlupin!

ALL: Long live Turlupin.

FLAVY: (aside) That insult! Never will I forget it.

TURLUPIN: Flatterers! They never applauded me so hard. Plainly, the King fills my role.

CHARLES: (turning towards him) What are you saying, Milord?

TURLUPIN: I am saying. I am saying, my master, that since you paint such good portraits, you owe us that of the Dauphin of France.

CHARLES: Say, the King, sir. Always, the King.

TURLUPIN: So be it, the King. Indeed, I am he. And if someone contests this title with me, at least I can count to make myself heard, with you, my lords, to whom I am giving a feast. Courage then, my Turlupin! Tell us a bit, in front of every one, what you think of the King of France.

CHARLES: Well—

SAINTRAILLES: (entering excitedly) Sire, Jeanne d'Arc of Domremy!

CHARLES: Jeanne of Arc!

SAINTRAILLES: The most humble, the most obscure of your subjects. But whose love of country raises her above all others. Through grace— You promised me, Sire. Do not refuse to hear her.

AGNES: (smiling) Isn't this young girl the one, who for the last three days, has ceaselessly presented herself at the gates of the Chateau, saying she's inspired by Heaven?

FLAVY and MARCILLAC: (laughing) By Heaven!

SAINTRAILLES: Don't laugh about it, Milords. You will soon be forced to recognize it.

AGNES: Tomorrow will be soon enough. Do the common people pursue their Kings right in the middle of their feasts?

CHARLES: Saintrailles. You heard her. Tomorrow—

TURLUPIN: (rising on the throne) No. Right now. This very instant.

ALL: Turlupin.

TURLUPIN: I am King, gentlemen! Everybody in his part. Mine is good and I'm keeping it. A young girl, a villager. That's news to us. Her presence, the naïveté of her speech are going to brighten up our feast. Let her come in. Such is our good pleasure.

ALL: (bursting into laughter) He's right. Let her come in!

SAINTRAILLES: Miserable buffoon! (to King) Mi-lord—

CHARLES: Let her enter. The King wills it. (Saintrailles hesitates. The King goes to shake his hand) The King wills it; go, my brave Saintrailles.

(Saintrailles crosses the stage. Joan, dressed as a man, appears in the exterior gallery. She stops mid-stage, eyes fixed on Turlupin on the throne. Then turns away as if looking for someone else.)

TURLUPIN: Approach, and speak without fear. The King indeed wishes to receive you. What do you have to say to him?

(Joan looks fixedly at him, mounts the steps of the throne, dominating Turlupin with her glance, forcing him to lower his eyes; then she takes off his crown, unhooks his royal cloak, draws the sword hanging at his side from its scabbard, and to the amazement of all takes the fool's cap from Charles, hurls it to the ground, then puts the sword in his hand.)

JEANNE: To arms! Milord, to arms! That's what the King of Heaven has ordered me to say to the King of France!

CHARLES: Who are you? And who taught you to recognize me, to single me out in the midst of all?

JEANNE: He who is sending me to lend aid to you and your kingdom; the one who orders you, through me, to be consecrated and crowned in the city of Rheims.

CHARLES: And who promised you that miracle?

JEANNE: Divine voices.

CHARLES: (smiling and placing the sword Joan has given him on the armchair) Ah, divine voices. You've heard them?

JEANNE: Often, Milord.

TURLUPIN: And in what language do they speak?

JEANNE: Better than yours.

CHARLES: And what did they tell you?

JEANNE: To go to the aid of the King of France and to return his kingdom to him.

CHARLES: Is that all? So, my dear child, you will do for me what neither Labire, nor Saintrailles, nor Dunois have been able to do? And can you give me no other sign of your mission?

FLAVY: Come on, Jeanne—just a little sign?

TURLUPIN: A little miracle.

JEANNE: I have not come here to test God, but to raise the siege of Orléans. Give me soldiers, many or few. I will go and I will do it. For, I tell you, Milord, that Saint Louis and Charlemagne are on their knees before God, praying for you.

CHARLES: (forcing more laughter) Ah, someone has prompted you about Saint Louis and Charlemagne.

TURLUPIN: (laughing with the others) Where the devil could she have gotten it?

(Joan appears beaten and desperate. Saintrailles alone tries to revive her look and impose silence on Turlupin. At this point, music representing the celestial voices can be heard in the midst of the courtiers' laughter.)

JEANNE: Milord, such were not your feelings, yesterday, in your oratory.

CHARLES: What do you mean? (the music stoops)

FLAVY: Very nice! She's going to tell the King his thoughts.

TURLUPIN: My loyal subjects, this is funny enough to be heard.

CHARLES: Think, Jeanne, what passed in me, yesterday. I haven't told anyone, not even my confessor. Speak now.

JEANNE: Sire, yesterday evening, (the music resumes) fallen into extreme discouragement, you made three requests of God. (the music stops)

TURLUPIN: You will see, they've been intercepted en route. (the music resumes)

JEANNE: First of all, you said, in your heart without uttering a word, "Lord God, if I am not the true heir of the noble house of France, take from me the courage to pursue an enterprise which costs so much blood to the Kingdom." (the music is again interrupted)

FLAVY: Is she going to advise the King to abandon—?

CHARLES: (suddenly serious) Silence, gentlemen. Continue Jeanne! (the music begins again)

JEANNE: "If this terrible calamity is because of my sins," you thought devotedly, "let me alone be struck, and the people of France be spared." (music ceases again)

FLAVY: This is really too much and we want—

CHARLES: (severely) Silence! (approaching Joan with kindness and a sort of terror) Jeanne, one thought—as it rose to God—did it add something? (final resumption of the music)

JEANNE: It said, "If my subjects, all powerful God, are alone guilty, pardon them, and take them in your mercy."

CHARLES: (moved, looking at Joan with enthusiasm and taking the sword from the armchair) To Orléans, gentlemen! To Orléans, I tell you. Jeanne is a messenger from God!

TURLUPIN: (to himself, taking up the fool's cap Joan threw at his feet) The King resumes his crown, I resume my fool's cap.

CHARLES: Jean Daulon, be her squire. You be her page.

Jeanne, take this banner.

JEANNE: (enthusiastically) I receive it from you, Sire, and I will return it only to God.

(The Lords quickly group around the King and Joan)

ALL: (general shout) To Orléans! To Orléans!

CURTAIN/BLACKOUT

ACT II

Scene 3: The Deliverance of Orléans

A street in Orléans a short distance from one of the main gates of the city. To the spectator's right, a barricade erected for the defense of the city.

AT RISE, a scene of despair and confusion. Noise of cannon bombarding the city. Women, old men, children are on their knees in several groups, hands extended to Heaven. A child of twelve is standing on the barricade, watching what is happening outside. The woman near him seems to be anxiously gesturing to him. The noise of the bombardment gradually ceases.

WOMAN: (to the child on the barricade) Well, what do you see? What's happening? Is the gate taken? Or are our soldiers still defending it?

CHILD: (frightened) Yes, still! They are closing in. They're fighting. They are killing each other.

WOMAN: Who's carrying the day?

CHILD: I don't know. I cannot make out. But the fighting is still in the same place.

OLD MAN: (on his knees) My God! My God! I've seen two of my sons perish. Won't you spare the only one who remains to me? Pity for us, my God! Pity for us!

ALL: Pity! Pity for us!

CHILD: (still atop the barricade) Ah! The banner of Talbot! Yes, I recognize it. And then the Count of Dunois, and then— Ah! (a shot is heard and the child falls, pierced by a ball)

WOMAN: (with a scream of despair, catching him in her arms) Ah, my child! Let the English take the city now— what's it to me? They've killed my child.

ALL: Let them come! Let them come!

(At this point the noise of the bombardment recommences. A group of people fall to their knees almost face against the ground. Other inhabitants enter fleeing, throwing their arms wildly.)

AN INHABITANT: It's all over! God is abandoning us. It wasn't enough to overturn our houses; from the height of their towers, they are directing their fire against the Cathedral tower.

OLD MAN: Soon we won't have any more asylum even in the churches.

AN INHABITANT: Let's all go to Talbot, offer him our hands. Demand mercy and grace from him. We will save our brothers who are still resisting him despite themselves. Come, don't wait for the English to reach us by marching over their cadavers. Follow me.

(All march to the left. Dunois enters with soldiers.)

DUNOIS: Halt! Where are you running to?

SEVERAL VOICES: The Count of DUNOIS!

INHABITANT: Milord, our misfortunes are overwhelming; our courage is exhausted.

DUNOIS: And you wish to give up? To fall at the knees of England?

INHABITANT: We want to save our children and our wives. Can France, which forgets us, order us to let them perish?

DUNOIS: France does not forget you. Haven't you been told that for the last two days in the neighboring countryside battles have taken place in which we've had the advantage. Battles led by a holy woman. Don't you believe any more in God who protects, or in the marvels that have been predicted to you?

INHABITANT: We are no longer thinking of anything except misery; of the horrible hunger which tortures us. (suddenly, a great uproar of voices)

DUNOIS: What's that? What's happening? Those confused voices? Those shouts?

INHABITANT: That crowd is rushing!

OLD MAN: Perhaps the English are masters of Orléans already?

DUNOIS: No! those are not shouts of distress and I recognize the banner of France.

ALL: The banner of France!

DURAND: (carried in triumph by the people) Yes, it is. And it's a woman who brings it to you.

ALL: A woman!

DURAND: It was indeed necessary that this happen. And the oracle has been accomplished.

ALL: The oracle.

DURAND: A woman ruined France. A virgin will save it.

ALL: A virgin!

DURAND: Yes, a young girl. A simple peasant. She's done more by herself alone. And she's more clever than all the gentlemen. Stronger than all the soldiers who surround her. With them, as he crossed the Loire; she fought the English; beat the mercenaries of Tyndal, Sack and Kill; she beat everybody. It's a blessing, what—through her, a convoy of supplies has just been introduced into Orléans. And here, look—look over there. (pointing) They are distributing bread to the inhabitants.

ALL: Bread.

DURAND: Jeanne of Arc is in their midst. Jeanne of Arc is coming to announce victory to you.

ALL: Jeanne of Arc.

DURAND: Here she is! Behold the daughter of God!

(Joan enters holding her banner in her hand. Near her, Saintrailles, then the Sire de Flavy, Marcillac, officers. Dunois and the inhabitants of Orléans surround Joan.)

JEANNE: (to Dunois) Milord, I've received from on high the order to share your perils and to be concerned like you with the safety of the country. You are a great prince and I am only a poor village girl. Nonetheless, God has told me we will be brothers in arms.

DUNOIS: Shake hands, whoever you may be. You speak

to me in the name of glory and the safety of France. You are giving bread to our unfortunate fellow citizens. Shake this hand and always count on me.

JEANNE: Time presses, the hour has come, we must prepare to fight.

DUNOIS: Fight and die.

JEANNE: No. Fight and conquer! Where are the principal forces of the English assembled?

DUNOIS: (pointing) Near the neighboring gate. Well! Let half of my men remain here, around this banner to defend the entrance to Orléans. It is necessary.

FLAVY: (low to Marcillac) Really, these are orders that she gives—

MARCILLAC: Let others follow them. As for me—

JEANNE: You all, Milords, you will share other important positions. It's for you to take by assault the four fortresses erected by the English around the city.

MARCILLAC: Take by assault!

FLAVY: Impossible!

JEANNE: Impossible! You have your opinion, gentlemen, and I have mine. (pointing to Heaven) The advice of the Lord is better than that of men. His will stand while yours will perish.

FLAVY: Believe blindly in this woman when the lives of so many brave men—

MARCILLAC: As for me, I will not submit.

JEANNE: Do so, gentlemen; and may Heaven not punish you. The battle will be terrible and my blood must be shed. But these knights will obey my voice and not yours. (addressing all) Have no doubt and march boldly! The hour has come that pleases God! He wants us to go forward and He holds Himself in readiness to aid us.

SAINTRAILLES: Yes, Jeanne d'Arc is our leader and we swear to obey her.

ALL: We swear it!

(A violent explosion outside. General disruption.)

JEANNE: (looking outside) Ah! What a frightful disaster.

DUNOIS: The Cathedral tower has just been knocked down!

JEANNE: The fire is coming from that bastion.

DUNOIS: The tower of Tournelles.

JEANNE: Who commands it?

DUNOIS: Tyndal, Sack and Kill.

ALL: Tyndal, Sack and Kill.

JEANNE: Who will take this man Jeanne's challenge and summons to surrender?

DUNOIS: I am prepared.

LABIRE: Here I am.

SAINTRAILLES: Order.

JEANNE: No. The presence of leaders is more useful elsewhere. And the one who is going to the fort of Tournelles is given to almost certain death.

DURAND: Well! me, Jeanne, if you wish it.

JEANNE: You, Durand?

DURAND: Why not? My life is such a little thing.

JEANNE: (with emotion) I confide your life to He who sends me.

SEVERAL MEN OF THE PEOPLE: I will follow him. And me, too.

JEANNE: Only two of you must follow him, and without arms. It's not as enemies you go to this man. (to Durand) You will ask to be introduced to him as a truce bearer. You will tell him that it is unjust and against the will of God for him to be master of this place. That within an hour I must plant my banner there. That the Lord has promised that to me. But, you will tell him that I have a horror of the blood which is going to be spilled, and that I conjure him to avoid that carnage and save all those who surround him.

DURAND: Goodbye, Jeanne.

JEANNE: (shaking his hand expressively) I will see you again. (Durand leaves, two men follow him) We will be ready to undertake the attack, Count Dunois. To you the most perilous position.

DUNOIS: Soldiers, to the West Tower. It must be taken by assault. (leaves with some men)

JEANNE: You, Count de Saintrailles; you will defend this gate with me.

SAINTRAILLES: (leaping on the barricade) I obey.

JEANNE: (to Baudricourt) You go to the fort of Saint Loup.

BAUDRICOURT: (to his soldiers) March.

JEANNE: (to another officer) You, to the bridge of the Loire.

OFFICER: (to his men) Follow me! (the three bands of soldiers each leave in different directions without interrupting the dialogue)

JEANNE: You, Mr. de Flavy—to the Burgundy gate.

FLAVY: Just a minute. As for me, I don't wish to obey.

MARCILLAC: Nor I—

JEANNE: (suddenly grasping Saintrailles' hand, Saintrailles is still on the barricade) Ah, Count, get down. Get down quickly. The place is cursed. (Saintrailles comes down, almost despite himself, dragged by Joan)

MARCILLAC: Mockery! As for me, I will take this station. (ascends the barricade)

FLAVY: (intending to follow him) And, me, too.

JEANNE: Stop! (shot from outside strikes Marcillac and causes him to fall off the barricade and roll to the feet of Flavy)

JEANNE: (resuming sadly) Too late! (to Flavy) Sir, to the Burgundy gate.

FLAVY: I obey. (leaves with his soldiers in the direction pointed out to him by Joan)

VOICES: (calling outside) Jeanne of Arc! Jeanne of Arc!

JEANNE: Who's calling me? (one of the men who left with Durand) Well! Are you returning alone? What have you to tell me?

MAN: The one who led us to the Fort of Tournelles—

JEANNE: Durand.— Finish!

MAN: He was taken and bound by the Freebooters and at this moment, perhaps, they've cut his throat.

JEANNE: My friend, my brother. Ah, let's run to defend him, if there is still time.

AN OFFICER: (at the barricade) The English! The English! They are entering the city. Here they are!

JEANNE: (rushing to the barricade and planting her flag) I am waiting for them! Courage, friends. Heaven's on our side and this place is ours!

(Firing. Then the English enter, coming to attack the barricade. Violent struggle. An all-out battle around Joan's flag. The English are repulsed.)

JEANNE: And now for the Fort of Tournelles!

ALL: To Tournelles! To Tournelles!

(At this point, an English soldier who has dragged himself, wounded, to the front of the stage, seems to regain his strength and aims at Joan of Arc. He fires; she falls in the arms of Saintrailles. They rush the English soldier but he collapses dead before they can reach him. All the French surround Joan, who has fainted in their arms. The music of celestial voices resumes. The Curtain Falls.

CURTAIN

ACT II

Scene 4: The Bastion of Tournelles

The top of the bastion whose interior can be seen is erected in the midst of the stage surrounded by an immense trench. To the spectators' left it communicates by a hanging bridge with another fortress.

AT RISE, the freebooters, harquebus in hand, seem to have successfully finished repulsing an attack, After several shots they rest their weapons. Durand is seated at the right. William is standing near him as if to prevent his escape.

DURAND: Do you think I am going to remain here a long while?

WILLIAM: A long while. That still wouldn't be too bad.

DURAND: Then, to distract me, give me some news. Three of us came. Why am I all alone?

WILLIAM: First of all, one of the other two fled.

DURAND: He didn't have a bad idea. And the other one?

WILLIAM: The other one noticed our leader at one of the loopholes.

DURAND: Tyndal, Sack and Kill.

WILLIAM: And he asked to speak to him, to be taken to him.

(Robert appearing to the left on the bridge which communicates from the other fortress)

ROBERT: (after coming across the bridge) Where is the prisoner?

WILLIAM: There he is.

ROBERT: (agitated) Ah, indeed!

WILLIAM: What's wrong with you?

ROBERT: What's wrong, is that this devil of a Tyndal has upset me.

WILLIAM: What do you mean?

ROBERT: Eh! yes— That man had asked to be led to the Captain; I escorted him. On the way, he said, to me laughing, "Ah, I'm not uneasy, we are old acquaintances, your chief and I."

WILLIAM: All that is not very terrifying.

ROBERT: We arrived. He went towards Tyndal, said a name to him that I didn't hear. Besides, I think he didn't have time to finish it, because the Captain split his head with his hatchet.

WILLIAM: The Devil! That's hasty, and this one here?

ROBERT: Ah! This one here. His business will soon be done. Tyndal wants to talk to him; he's coming.

WILLIAM: (brutally, to Durand) Come here, you!

DURAND: What do they want with me?

ROBERT: You'll find out soon enough.

WILLIAM: On your knees! (William and Robert force him to kneel)

DURAND: As you will, so long as this is soon over.

(Tyndal crosses the bridge, hatchet in hand, and comes forward looking furious towards Durand)

FREEBOOTERS: (bowing) The Captain.

TYNDAL: (to his soldiers) Get Back. (They all go toward the back of the bastion. Tyndal comes to Durand who rises.) Where are you from?

DURAND: From little Burcy near Domremy.

TYNDAL: Do you recognize me?

DURAND: No. I am not linked to any wild beast.

TYNDAL: I will know if you are lying. What is the first house in Domremy, when entered from the woods of Chenu?

DURAND: Heavens! You were with those who pillaged us two years ago.

TYNDAL: Answer!

DURAND: It's the house of mother Tiphaine.

TYNDAL: (with emotion) She's still alive?

DURAND: She was still there when I left the first time— that was six weeks ago. The brave woman.

TYNDAL: (aside) My mother. (aloud) And what did you come to do here?

DURAND: To accompany Jeanne.

TYNDAL: Jeanne the Sorceress.

DURAND: Jeanne of Arc.

TYNDAL: Jeanne of Arc! Did you say? What! That girl they call the witch could be—

DURAND: The daughter of my uncle Jacques.

TYNDAL: (aside) She, so near me. Ah! I will have my prey. (aloud) To me, my freebooters!

DURAND: What's making you so angry?

TYNDAL: Your weapons, comrades, your best weapons, your most terrible audacity. Climb down these walls, cross this moat. At the gate of Orléans is a woman that must be captured. I must have her, I tell you.

A FREEBOOTER: Jeanne the Sorceress! The Devil's Daughter! (terror amongst all)

TYNDAL: There is no magic! There is no devil! There's only a woman that I want to capture; that I want to hold here, in my power. On whom I intend to avenge you; you, me, England. (all move away from Tyndal) You hesitate, cowardly brigands!

(William reappears on the bridge from which he addresses the Captain.)

WILLIAM: Great news, Captain. The spell is broken. Hell no longer fights against us.— The witch—

TYNDAL and THE FREEBOOTERS: Well?

WILLIAM: Here, see down there. That funeral cortege; those standards covered in a black veil. And all those warriors on their knees before the witch—who is no longer to be feared. She is dead.

ALL: Dead!

TYNDAL: Dead! And I've neither possessed her, nor killed her.

DURAND: Dead! Kill me! Kill me, I want to rejoin her.

TYNDAL: And, as for me, I am too happy now to think of raising the axe again over your head. I grant you mercy. Get out!

DURAND: I don't want to go. I want to be killed.

TYNDAL: Be gone, I tell you.

DURAND: No. Let them kill me. What must I do to decide you? Rogue! Brigand! Murderer! Isn't that enough? What further insult must I address to you?

TYNDAL: Well— Throw him in the moat.

(Freebooters seize Durand and toss him from the top of the rampart into the moat. Then they all look over the rampart.)

TYNDAL: Well?

WILLIAM: Escaped! He swims like a cork.

TYNDAL: (aside) Dead! Well—so much the better! Jealous rage will no longer burn in my heart. Let's drink comrades. Flagons, cups.

(Some mercenaries place cups on a table. At this point Robert reappears on the bridge.)

ROBERT: Captain! Captain! To arms! (all the men drop their cups and rush to take up arms)

GENERAL SHOUT: To arms!

ROBERT: (excitedly) The Count of Dunois is at the foot of the Bastille of Saint Loup. (pointing to the adjoining fort) It must be defended.

TYNDAL: No. It's unnecessary. An old dismantled fort that contains neither supplies nor munitions. Let Dunois' troop waste its time seizing it, and you, comrades, rally around me in this bastion.

ROBERT: But Dunois, once master of the Fort, is going to cross the bridge with his soldiers and then—

TYNDAL: Then—that's where I'll be waiting for him. (taking his hatchet he rushes the bridge, striking at various points, then detaches the rings of several chains which support the bridge and rushes back to the bastion of Tournelles)

WILLIAM: What have you done, Captain?

TYNDAL: Now let Dunois come and let him try to cross the bridge. (bursting into laughter) Ha! ha! ha! ha! (all the mercenaries burst into ferocious laughter)

GENERAL SHOUT: Long live Tyndal, Sack and Kill. Long live our Captain! (all the soldiers lay aside their arms and go back to the table and resume their drinking)

TYNDAL: Let's rejoice and no longer fear either Dunois or his companions in arms. They no longer have that which gave them strength, that which rendered them invincible. Ha, ha, ha! They lost their sorceress. (new bursts of laughter, much drinking)

WILLIAM: That woman. Did you see her, Captain?

TYNDAL: Yes, I've seen her. I knew her. And for a long while yet—

WILLIAM: Was she beautiful?

TYNDAL: Beautiful enough to tempt the most chaste of men. Beautiful! And indeed, that's what made her conquer. It's her beauty, her beauty alone, which enflames the hearts around her, which gave so much courage to all the knights.

ROBERT: Yes, without doubt. Her beauty and the power of Satan.

TYNDAL: (rising) Satan! Ha! ha! ha! You believe that, you, Robert?

WILLIAM: And you don't believe it, Captain?

TYNDAL: I believe in nothing. Nothing except what I can touch. Nothing except what I can hold. In my axe, in my cup. So long as there remains wine for me to fill it with. Come, pour!

WILLIAM: Now there's a worthy Captain! He will dance on the tomb of his mother.

TYNDAL: (rising in the greatest agitation) Of my mother! (taking up his hatchet and rushing on William, furiously throwing him to the ground) Who told you that?

WILLIAM: (trembling) Don't you hate the whole universe?

TYNDAL: You think there is fury only in hate? No, no— it's not hate which hurls this hot agitation in us, these desires, these impotent rages, dog that you are! I tell you it's not hate. (tossing away his axe and moving away from William who rises) Let's drink! We must drink since she's dead! Drink to her death! And let our shouts of joy reach those who weep for her. To the death of the witch!

GENERAL SHOUT: To the death of the sorceress!

(As they drink this toast, they turn towards the French camp. But at this moment Joan appears on the summit of the bastion, banner in hand. Dunois and Saintrailles are next to her. And, in an instant, all the loopholes are filled on the right with French soldiers who have scaled the fortress, and who aim at Tyndal and his soldiers. General shouts among the Freebooters.)

ALL: Ah! It's her! She's a ghost, a spectre. Let's get out of here.

(The French fire on the Freebooters. Others take refuge on the bridge. Tyndal seems to struggle against the intoxication and involuntary terror that this apparition inspires in him. Putting his hand to his side and realizing he has no weapon, he takes two steps back despite himself.)

TYNDAL: Unarmed! Unarmed!

(Robert and William try to drag him through a small gate on the extreme left. The mercenaries who have tried to reach the bridge find it occupied by Dunois and his soldiers. Tyndal's band is fired on from the right and the left. Then the bridge collapses and they fall uttering screams of despair. The fortress of Tournelles is invaded on all sides by the French Army which groups around Joan.

GENERAL SHOUT: Long live France! Long live the King! Long live the Maid!

CURTAIN

ACT III

Scene 5: The Consecration at Rheims

The Cathedral Square. The Cathedral's portal is visible. Houses on both sides of the stage. To the left, a street. To the right, another street next to the Cathedral. On the left, a house where Jeanne is lodging. On the right, another house with a barred window on the street floor.

AT RISE, the stage is filled with town and country folk who jostle each other, looking down the street to the left.

A MAN OF THE PEOPLE: (to a Bourgeois) Will it be soon?

BOURGEOIS: It's more than an hour since they brought the Holy Oil from the Abbey of Saint Remi to the Cathedral, and an upholsterer, who just left, told me that the archbishop, with the clergy, was awaiting the King at the altar.

(Soldiers enter and push the crowd into two files; meanwhile, Durand enters, supporting Louise, who appears exhausted by fatigue, and directs her to Joan's house.)

DURAND: Courage, Louise! We're here on time. The procession is going to pass, and here's the house where my old pal Chartrin has retained rooms for me.

LOUISE: Ah, I can't do any more; but it's all the same. To see the procession will revive my strength. How many people! With this crowd, I won't be able to see anything.

DURAND: Wait! (to a man of the people who is atop a milestone at a corner near the Cathedral) Say, my brave man, would you, who are tall, give your place to me?

MAN: My place. (addressing his comrades, who are hanging from a corner of the balcony) Say, Gardouillot, here's a gentleman who is asking me if I'd give him my place. Tell him for me, it cannot be done.

DURAND: (to Louise) Now there's what it is to be dressed like a peasant. Say, man—?

MAN: Gardouillot, do you know what this lord wants?

DURAND: The place to put my foot. Just one. Beside yours.

MAN: Gardouillot, tell his lordship that his foot is too big.

DURAND: But it's not for me; it's for a young girl.

MAN: A young girl, that suits! Come up, my pretty child. Next to me. (Louise puts one foot on the milestone, the other on the transept)

DURAND: Thanks, my brave man. (to Louise) Are you set? Hold on to my shoulder.

(The procession emerges from the street and crosses the stage diagonally—successively, guards, heralds, lords, then Labire, Saintrailles, Dunois, King Charles, Joan.)

LOUISE: (to Durand) But, you can't see?

DURAND: I'm standing on tiptoe. (Movement in the crowd. Shouts "Long live the King!") Great! There they are, right in front of me, and I can no longer see a thing.

LOUISE: Say, Durand? there's the King! There's the King!

DURAND: Oh! I know him. Go away. Well! look beside him. Don't you see anything?

LOUISE: A handsome warrior who seems quite young. He's carrying a banner.

DURAND: Do you see his face?

LOUISE: No. He's turning his face the other way. Ah!

My God!

DURAND: What's wrong?

LOUISE: He's looking! It's (calling) Jeannette! (Durand moves, Louise falls on her feet to the ground)

DURAND: Would you please quiet down. (Joan looks about, sees nothing and continues to march) Are you silly to disturb the procession like that? Ah, you think things are done this way. That you just scream aloud: "Jeannette." Well, I have only to call from a distance King Charles. That would have been a fine coronation.

LOUISE: But I haven't seen her for so long—

DURAND: But, be patient. You don't have the last idea what a court is like. (The procession enters the Cathedral) Go rest a bit in my room. I will put on my soldier's clothes and that way I will get near her. Come on, come on, I tell you there's no more to be seen.

(The people lay siege to the approaches to the cathedral. The troops forming barriers are grouped to the right. Durand and Louise go into the house.)

FLAVY: (entering, to the officer commanding the troops) Place your soldiers beneath the balcony of the Archbishop where the King will soon appear after the coronation. Then, you go to the advance posts leading to the Paris gates and you will inform yourself of the movements of the enemy. If they make some hostile demonstration, you will come inform me of it. Do you hear? To me alone.

(The officer retires to the right. As Flavy watches him go, D'Estivet emerges from a group he was mingled in and approaches Flavy.)

FLAVY: You here, D'Estivet.

D'ESTIVET: Wherever my cause calls me.

FLAVY: That of Burgundy or England?

D'ESTIVET: That of Heaven.

FLAVY: Of Heaven you say?

D'ESTIVET: You, Guillaume de Flavy; are you too subjugated by the witchcraft of this enemy of God?

FLAVY: I submitted to her genius and it's quite enough. Twenty times I wanted to rebel against her ascendancy; twenty times she seemed to call on a miracle to confound me. I opposed risking a set battle; she attacks the English at Patay, crosses swords with the great Talbot and takes him prisoner. To lead the King from Orléans to Rheims, I shouted and repeated that we had to do eighty leagues through enemy territory, take three great towns, Auxerre, Troyes, Chalons, and that we lacked supplies. Auxerre regained its freedom as soon as it saw the army. Troyes demanded mercy. And the bishop of Chalons came to bring the King the keys to the city.

D'ESTIVET: And in reward of this opposition which is always defeated, the King has relegated you to Compiegne, where he leaves you in command to console you for your disgrace.

FLAVY: At least I won't see her any more.

D'ESTIVET: A feeble vengeance. To be satisfied with fleeing the sight of the enemy.

FLAVY: What do you want from me?

D'ESTIVET: That you join in our holy efforts.

FLAVY: To betray King Charles!

D'ESTIVET: No. To repudiate the aid of a limb of Satan. Our vengeance is approaching. The woman appears to you in the high point of glory. It's the high point indeed, for her. She's going to come down. It's no longer only on the field of battle she will have to fight. Jealousy is spreading from your heart to the hearts of twenty leaders. Perhaps the King, himself, who is satiated with her to the point of disgust. The clergy is ready to shout anathema against her; a terrible adversary, Tyndal, Sack and Kill has sworn to avenge on her the shame of his flight and defeat. The University of Paris is condemning her. The inquisition awaits her at its tribunal! You alone—will you forget the offenses against Heaven and yourself?

FLAVY: No. I remember she chased my mistress who was following me out of camp.

D'ESTIVET: Her morals will be proclaimed damnable and her life evil.

FLAVY: She has accused me of pillaging.

D'ESTIVET: We will have witnesses to prove that she was cruel and murderous.

FLAVY: Because of her, I am called impious.

D'ESTIVET: As for us, we will call her scandalous and blasphemous.

FLAVY: What do you need for this?

D'ESTIVET: The promise of serving us against her when the day comes.

(A group of people leaves the porch of the Cathedral crossing the stage shouting: "To the Archbishop's!")

FLAVY: My service calls me to the King.

D'ESTIVET: (retaining him) First, answer. Will you be with us?

FLAVY: No. But I swear to you, I will be against her.

D'ESTIVET: You will see me again, the day it is necessary to act.

(Flavy leaves by the right; D'Estivet, by the left. The window in the house by the right opens. Durand dressed as in Scene III comes out of the house and approaches the barred window.)

DURAND: Stay there. I am going to try to rejoin you. As soon as I've found her, I will come to warn you. The ceremony must be advanced by now. (a second wave of people rushing) Oh! Now there are the folks coming back from the church and going under the windows of the Archbishop. (accosting the man he spoke to earlier) Say, there. Hey, man! Were you in the Cathedral?

MAN: Partly.

DURAND: Huh?

MAN: Yes. Only my head was inside. The rest was outside on the shoulders of Gardouillot.

DURAND: Well, what did you see?

MAN: Everything! I saw the King go to the altar. They put oil from the blessed ampoule on his face, then they put a crown on him.

DURAND: And Jeanne of Arc?

MAN: Heavens! You are like all those who were beneath me and who were also asking, "And Jeanne of Arc?"

DURAND: And you replied to them?

MAN: I told them "There she is by the altar, to the right of the King. She's holding her banner. Everybody is rising to see her. No one is so much as looking at the Queen. Come on, the rest of you! (he exits—everyone follows)

DURAND: That's it. I'm going to wait here for her to leave. (Joan leaves the church, followed by a page carrying her banner)

JEANNE: (noticing Durand) Durand! You, my friend!

DURAND: (confused) You call me your friend. With such a beautiful helmet and plume. (as he speaks, Joan gives her page her helmet, scarf and sword)

JEANNE: Take these arms to my lodging and prepare everything as I told you. (the page goes into the house on the left)

DURAND: You left the ceremony. The King, the Archbishop?

JEANNE: (returning to him) Durand, you deserted.

DURAND: (terrified) Me, my God!

JEANNE: You deserted! You were thinking of it already when we left Troyes, but when we arrived at Chalons you disappeared and here it is five days since I've seen you.

DURAND: I was wrong, I was wrong. But you didn't know.

JEANNE: Oh, yes, I knew! You said to yourself, "Ah, near the chalk fields of Champagne there's a country of beautiful pasturages and forests. This country is called Lorraine, and by marching one whole day and one whole night I can be in Domremy."

DURAND: (overwhelmed.) Well! It's true.

JEANNE: (heatedly) You went to Domremy! You saw my mother, my father, my sisters, my friends. Oh, come. Speak to me of them, paint their faces for me, tell me their words. Despite all the distance, in the heart at least, I see them and hear them!

DURAND: Then you haven't forgotten?

JEANNE: Forget Domremy, Vaucouleurs, the woods of Chenu? I, too, when near Chalons, I felt the air coming from Lorraine. Air that had passed through our trees, perhaps. I was gripped by such a love of country that with both hands I restrained my horse, for fear, divining my thoughts, it would take me to Domremy. But mother! My mother?

DURAND: She was suffering a bit from sadness.

JEANNE: Ill!

DURAND: So she couldn't come.

JEANNE: She wanted to come?

DURAND: Yes. And in her place—

JEANNE: Who then?

DURAND: Louise.

LOUISE: (rushing in) Oh, my Jeannette.

JEANNE: (holding her in her arms) You! You! My Louise. My good sister!

LOUISE: You love us then?

JEANNE: Yes, I love you! Mother is ill?

LOUISE: She's going to be better when she has some news of you.

JEANNE: And father?

LOUISE: He's proud of you now.

JEANNE: And Marguerite?

LOUISE: She's married.

JEANNE: Happily?

LOUISE: Quite happily.

JEANNE: And the neighbors and La Haumette and her child who was sick?

LOUISE: Everybody is fine. Very fine!

JEANNE: Ah! It's nice to say all those names. And tell me, the crop— is it good?

LOUISE: At least ten more sacks than last year.

JEANNE: Oh, look at me. So I can get a good look at you, so I can see all those who are absent through you. It's really you. See, Durand, how her eyes are like my father's. Heavens, and my mother's smile when she was pleased with me. Oh, I embrace you again.

LOUISE: And Durand was afraid.

JEANNE: Afraid of what?

LOUISE: He forbade me to call you just now when you

went by.

JEANNE: You were there? It was you I heard?

LOUISE: He said you no longer spoke to him of us.

DURAND: Oh!!! I don't accuse you. Only this hurts me. And I said, she's no longer of this earth, and all those who remain are indeed little to her.

JEANNE: Was I that way? I didn't even know it. My mission filled my soul completely. I felt I was living for the safety of many men, and the divine inspiration raised me to mine and to myself. But to the degree the celestial task has been accomplished, I felt the need to see you return, to be what I once was, and with each step that approached Rheims I became daughter and sister again.

DURAND: (timidly) And not something more.

JEANNE: (offering him her hand) Friend.

DURAND: (aside, sadly) The rest welcome, perhaps, later.

LOUISE: Jeannette, mother has charged me to ask you something.

DURAND: Not now, Louise, not now.

LOUISE: Why's that?

DURAND: If you consecrate a King, you think that you would have a head for what they come to tell you. You are not discreet, Louise, you are not discreet.

JEANNE: (to Louise) Speak anyway.

LOUISE: Mother told me to ask you when you could come to see her.

JEANNE: When, Louise, when—?

DURAND: (noticing Saintrailles leaving the church) The Count Saintrailles.

JEANNE: Here, Louise, go into this house. You will find a page making preparations that you understand better than he and who will tell you my reply. Go. I will rejoin you in a moment.

LOUISE: (as she is about to enter, to Durand) Are you coming with me?

DURAND: It's such a long time since I've seen her.

LOUISE: (laughing) Wait there then, since she's going to come, too.

(Exit Louise)

SAINTRAILLES: Jeanne, at the moment when the King was presenting himself to the acclamations of the people, I sought you near him. Everyone was looking for you, as I was. You weren't there, And yet, in the presence of the King, in the presence of all, I had to speak to you, Jeanne.

JEANNE: I am ready to hear you everywhere, Count de Saintrailles.

SAINTRAILLES: It seems to me that my words won't have the solemnity I want for them. Tomorrow, at the foot of the throne.

JEANNE: No, lord, this very day, I ask it of you. Tomorrow, perhaps we will be separated.

SAINTRAILLES: What! An order of the King?

JEANNE: (smiling) More than that.

SAINTRAILLES: Your divine voices?

JEANNE: Speak. I am listening to you.

SAINTRAILLES: We are in the presence of these sacred walls where you've just accomplished the great work that you announced three months ago and which no one wanted to believe. During those three months, I have always been near you. I've seen your indomitable courage in battle; I've seen your sweetness and your pity after victory. I've seen you lay aside your holy banner to care for the enemy wounded.

DURAND: (aside) Oh. He loves her the way the people love her.

JEANNE: I am happy you didn't tell me these things before the court.

SAINTRAILLES: What I wanted to proclaim before the whole court, before the entire universe is that so much simplicity and grandeur have not only filled my heart with admiration, but also with the most tender devotion, the purest passion—

DURAND: (aside) Oh. He loves her too much! He loves her too much.

JEANNE: Count!

SAINTRAILLES: Oh! Fear nothing. I know all the respect your chaste and holy life merit; also it was in presence of the altar, where just now the King was consecrated that Saintrailles wanted to offer you his name, his rank, his life!

DURAND: (aside) Ah, as for me I cannot say that.

SAINTRAILLES: Jeanne—you don't respond.

JEANNE: I thank God for having placed me between two

such noble natures.

SAINTRAILLES: What are you saying?

JEANNE: You, one of the first men of the Court after King Charles VII, you are offering me your name without fear of mockery, without suspecting that jealousy which is secretly arming itself, against which you wish to offer me support—that's true nobility, Count Saintrailles; that's grandeur.

SAINTRAILLES: That's love.

DURAND: (aside) Oh, my God—how he says that word!

JEANNE: And, now, I have here, at my side, a man who's known me since my birth, with whom I played as a child in my village.

DURAND: (aside) Can she be speaking of me?

JEANNE: He detested war; he followed me. He fought beside me. He's been valiant, devoted. And when there was a moment that I took him away from the land in which we'd grown up together, I felt in his voice, for no word betrayed him, I felt that, what you just said to me, he also felt.

DURAND: (aside) It was her voices that told her.

SAINTRAILLES: Yes, Jeanne, People and nobility, all

must adore you. It's up to you to choose.

JEANNE: Prince, what God, in his anger or in his bounty, has marked with His finger belongs to Him.

SAINTRAILLES: That decree we cannot accept.

JEANNE: Saintrailles, if one day my name is remembered, they will speak at the same time of yours. And because of what you have done for France, and because of what you have done for me—I love you as a sister. I can love no other way. And if Heaven has left a place in my heart for any other affection, that glory of which you speak, that glory of a girl of the people: I have not the will to steal it from the people.

SAINTRAILLES: What are you saying?

JEANNE: And I would have borne in dowry to my equal, who has been able to speak to me of my mother, of my family, and of loving them with me.

(Durand comes to her, and on his knees kisses the hem of her coat of mail.)

SAINTRAILLES: Jeanne you are noble and simple to the point of despair. And you must be admired even more.

(music announcing the return of the procession)

JEANNE: Here's the return of the Royal Procession.

Goodbye, Saintrailles, goodbye, my brother in arms. (going towards the house at the left she finds herself near Durand, to whom she extends her hand)

DURAND: (transported with joy) Come, it's all the same. I am still happier than a prince. (He follows Joan into the house. The King, followed by his gentlemen emerges from the Cathedral.)

KING: Saintrailles, have you ordered our King of Arms to be here?

SAINTRAILLES: Milord, King, here he is with maps and parchments you told him to bring.

KING: (looking about) Isn't Jeanne of Arc with us?

SAINTRAILLES: (pointing to the house) She just retired to her lodgings.

KING: Her modesty will not escape our gratitude. Saintrailles, go capture her and bring her to us. Announce to her our intentions, which you are aware of. (to King of Arms) And now, proclaim what is my will.

KING OF ARMS: (after a trumpet call) Charles, the Seventh of that name, by the Grace of God, King of France, to render glory to the high and divine wisdom of numerous graces that it has pleased God to shower on him through the ministry of his dear and well beloved Jeanne of Arc of Domremy grants letters of nobility to the aforesaid Jeanne and all of hers and by a special exception wills that this nobility with its titles and privileges which are attached to it, belong also in this family to the feminine descendants, in memory of the young girl who saved Orléans. Jeanne of Arc and hers are authorized to take in their arms the lily of France and the escutcheon shall be placed above the house of Jacques d'Arc in Domremy.

(The people shout with enthusiasm "Long Live the King!" The lords keep silent. Movement in the crowd which is agitated, murmuring "Jeanne! Jeanne! Here she comes! Here she comes!")

SAINTRAILLES: (coming out of the house) Milord, Jeanne is coming at your orders. (Joan emerges in the costume of a peasant girl accompanied by Louise and Durand.)

KING: (seeing Joan's costume) What's this mean?

JEANNE: (falling to her knees) Milord, pardon me.

KING: Saintrailles— Haven't you told her that our bounty—?

JEANNE: Milord, I have to ask of you a thing more precious to me than gold and nobility.

KING: What's that?

JEANNE: Permission to return to Domremy.

(General consternation)

KING: Do you want me to be accused of ingratitude? A place near the throne is designated for she who helped to restore the throne.

JEANNE: Milord, if I have previously obeyed the orders of Heaven, if I have completed the mission imposed upon me— Don't punish me. Don't make me a prisoner in your court. I don't know how to live here. With divine help I was hardly able. What will become of me now that I am here before this holy church whose gate is the only way open to me? Milord, by divine will I confronted war, I saw many wounded and dying. I had blood on my feet and on my hands. And you told me that I was harvesting glory. Well, glory is not what I need. What I need is my country, my mother, and him, the man who rejected me and hasn't hugged me since the day of my departure—my poor father. Oh, let me leave, let me see him again. Here, this is my sister who came from my country with my cousin. She told me that my mother weeps. And as for me, I call her, I need her. I need my original life. If you wish it, believe Milord, believe that it's I who gave you France and the crown. Believe it, and in return, return me my village, return me my happiness, return me my mother.

LOUISE: Ah! You are right to love her, Durand.

DURAND: The whole world knows my secret now!

SAINTRAILLES: Jeanne, have you no regret in separating from your brothers in arms?

DUNOIS and SAINTRAILLES: (bowing before her) Stay! oh, stay!

FLAVY: You will see that they will keep her and that the King cannot do anything without her.

(Saintrailles and Dunois appear to beg Joan. The people are on their knees. Durand and Louise are uneasy and signal Joan to follow them.)

KING: (after a moment of silence) Jeanne, you will it. I won't keep you any longer. Despite the regret I feel.

JEANNE: Ah! Heaven will finish for you what it only began with me. (to Louise and Durand) Sister, Durand, now everything is yours.

DURAND: (removing his armor and buckler) Since now there are lands where one can farm without fear of the English, I resume the plough.

KING: Jeanne. Don't you wish to ask anything of the King before leaving him?

JEANNE: Milord, if you wish. I would really like to honor Domremy.

KING: What must be done for it?

JEANNE: Domremy is on the frontier. It has been pillaged often. If I could announce it was exempt from duties and war taxes—

KING: You may announce it.

JEANNE: Thanks, Milord, and God protect the King! God protect France.

(Dunois and Saintrailles go to Joan to say their goodbyes. An officer enters, finds Flavy, and goes rapidly to him.)

FLAVY: (low) What's the matter?

OFFICER: (low) The English. Instead of withdrawing—

FLAVY: (low) Not a word! (aside) They'll think they have need of her!

JEANNE: Durand, you know the way: take us to Domremy.

KING: And as for us, Milords, we are going to complete the conquest of France.

FLAVY and SEVERAL LORDS: Long live the King!

ALL THE PEOPLE: Glory to Jeanne!
CURTAIN

ACT IV

Scene 6: Compeigne or Treason

The stage represents a four-way crossroads entering Compeigne. In the rear, slanted towards the right, town walls with a large gate. Drawbridges over the moat separating the town from the city. To the right, a small chapel with a bench under the statue of a saint.

AT RISE, distant acclamations can be heard, and the noise of bells. D'Estivet, leaning against a tree, looks at Sire de Flavy who listens uneasily to those noises and goes to the moat to hear better.

D'ESTIVET: Flavy, listen carefully to the ringing bells and those acclamations that are moving into the distance. And if they don't speak loud enough, I shall take care to revive their meaning in your ears. Those bells say that Compeigne, besieged by the English and defended for the last six months by Sire de Flavy has just been aided by Jeanne of Arc. Those acclamations repeat that Sire de Flavy wasn't a warrior sufficiently valiant, a leader significantly clever to raise the siege. And that a young girl without troops, without strength, is going to deliver the city and steal from de Flavy the honor of its long defense. (As D'Estivet speaks, Flavy gives an order to a soldier near a parapet by the moat and the soldier returns into the city.)

FLAVY: (coming to D'Estivet) Do you think nothing in me says what you believe you are revealing to me? Did I dissimulate my joy when, at Rheims, I thought she went to hide the glory she had stolen from us in Domremy, content henceforth to amuse the evening bedtime hours of her village with her exploits—that soon would be no more than an apocryphal legend in the depths of Lorraine? Did I dissimulate my scorn and chagrin when the people, terrified by the English, threw themselves at her feet and bathed them with tears? Fanatical imbeciles! And today, because at break of day she's entering into Compeigne, as soon as she put herself at the head of a sortie I commanded, they forget that my arm protected their ramparts for the last six months, while this mad woman wandered about the center of France.

D'ESTIVET: Yes, you understand well enough the insults you've received. And yet you still hesitate to make common cause with us. You remain enslaved to the cause of this King, your old companion in pleasures, who is sacrificing you to this adventuress. And soon, Captain, saved by a young strip of a girl, you'll have nothing better to do than to follow her as a faithful and grateful retainer. And since another already bears her sword and her lance, you could bear her peasant cot from Lorraine until the day when someone better advised than you will force her to take it back.

FLAVY: Enough! Enough! Finally, I can answer you. You see that man coming?

D'ESTIVET: Who is he?

FLAVY: He's the guardian of this gate.

D'ESTIVET: Then we can count on you?

FLAVY: Listen! (to Guardian) Come forward. How much time is required to lower the portcullis and raise this bridge?

GUARDIAN: Less than a minute, my lord.

FLAVY: From your post, can you distinguish in the midst of the noise of musketry a cannon shot from the square tower?

GUARDIAN: I am certain of not making a mistake.

FLAVY: Listen then; for on your life you will answer for the execution of the order I am going to give you.

GUARDIAN: On my life, I will obey, Milord.

FLAVY: At some moment you will hear the cannon of the

square tower, Then let the men who remain on this side of the moat lower the portcullis, raise the bridge and be dumb to all prayers, to all command.

GUARDIAN: At the smoke from the cannon's mouth, no one can enter the town.

FLAVY: Right! To your post. (the Guardian leaves) I can see all that is happening outside the town. I'm going to wait.

D'ESTIVET: And as for me, I am going to bring your reply to those who sent me. Orders are given everywhere and at the signal we will be ready.

(Flavy enters into the city. D'Estivet leaves by the right. To the left, Durand enters supporting Joan, carrying her banner. Joan holds in her hand her broken sword and appears exhausted with fatigue. Durand makes her sit on the stone bench and places her banner against a tree.)

DURAND: Jeanne! Jeanne! What's wrong with you? Why this despondency? Why have you left the battlefield? Are we then in flight?

JEANNE: We are victors. We are pursuing the enemy, who's been routed.

DURAND: Why then so lacking in strength? Tired, perhaps?

JEANNE: It seems to me there will be a misfortune.

DURAND: Where?

JEANNE: On us.

DURAND: Compeigne will be taken?

JEANNE: No, not Compeigne.

DURAND: What then?

JEANNE: I don't know.

DURAND: Me, either, I don't know, Jeanne. But I remember the day when this sadness came to you.

JEANNE: You noticed?

DURAND: We were fighting around Melun and you had been valiant, as always, shouting to us, "Push forward, they are yours!" Suddenly, you stopped; you seemed to listen to noises we didn't hear, you became pale, and, often after that, I've seen you dazed and overwhelmed.

JEANNE: That's really it.

DURAND: Is it because on that day you were in fear, Jeanne?

JEANNE: Yes.

DURAND: Afraid to die?

JEANNE: No—

DURAND: If not to die, what's there to be afraid of?

JEANNE: Of the tidings announced to me.

DURAND: What tidings?

JEANNE: That I will be taken by the English.

DURAND: You, Jeanne! By them!

JEANNE: Yes, and I would much rather be dead.

DURAND: Did you just now run some danger of it?

JEANNE: Just now it seemed to me that the blood drained from my heart. My sword, the sword that Saint Catherine made me find behind the altar of the Virgin of Fierbois; this sword broke in my hand. (letting herself fall) Ah, it's because the divine breath has ceased to carry me, you see, I am falling back into life and its weaknesses.

DURAND: Ah! My God! If they knew—!

JEANNE: Oh shut up! Especially, shut up!

DURAND: Yes, I will shut up, Jeanne. For the rest of us, what will become of us if we were to lose the faith we have in you? We are going into battle without knowing anything. We start to kill when they tell us. And we kill those where they put us. To have a little ardor in dying we need at least, to love those who command us. And we love you, Jeanne, because we know that you are leading us to war not through pride, not through vengeance, but to prevent them from pillaging our fields, so they don't violate our mothers and our sisters; we understand that. And we feel that you are for France. And we are ready to perish for you, saying, "She must live to save those who remain." Jeanne, don't take from us our confidence and our courage.

JEANNE: You're right, Durand. I don't have the right to be weak. I owe myself to those who are obeying me, and if they themselves were threatened by the misfortune I feel is coming. If some ambush— Listen, Durand, cross the Oise on a boat you will find near here. Try to rejoin the Sire de Flavy or one of his lieutenants. Let the order be given not to pursue the enemy further. It's necessary to come back.

DURAND: You become Captain, again, I become soldier again. (goes out to the left)

JEANNE: (alone) I am trying vainly to sustain the power which dismays me. I feel a great sorrow coming to me. Forgive me, my weakness, my God! Your divine son, knowing that a man delivered and betrayed him, said to you, "Lord take this cup from me." As for me, that you have chosen, I dare to make the same prayer to you as the Saviour of all. "Spare me this cup of bitterness." But, if it's one of your absolute laws that whoever chosen by you must, for purification, accept the suffering, if misfortune alone can consecrate the weak in the eyes of men, my God! Here I am ready and resigned. I ask no more of you than to keep my mother unaware of it. And to give me the strength to suffer it with dignity. (music of the celestial voices) Ah, again! again! It's no longer victory you are announcing to me now. The day of trials has come. I am ready for them. What do I hear? It would be better for me when two o'clock strikes to be within the walls of Compeigne—would be better. Ah, I obey, you Lord. Let's go in!

(She goes towards the tree where her banner is, to take it. But entering from the left French soldiers are brutally escorting prisoners to the drawbridge. One of them who throws himself before Joan is young Talbot, wounded.)

SOLDIER: Move, I tell you. Do you think I'm going to let you fall behind?

TALBOT: You see I am wounded and that I can hardly drag myself. (Joan stops)

SOLDIER: All the same, I advise you to move, if not—

TALBOT: (with effort) I cannot.

SOLDIER: Then so much the worse. (striking him with

his sword.)

(Talbot falls.)

JEANNE: (coming forward) Miserable coward! To strike a prisoner. An injured man.

SOLDIER and ALL WHO SURROUND HIM: Jeanne of Arc. (they bow with respect)

FRENCH OFFICER: (coming out of the town and stopping on the drawbridge) Soldiers! Hasten to reenter the city.... Push the stragglers. Make the prisoners march.

(The French and the prisoners reenter the town. Joan has hurried to assist Talbot who has fainted.)

JEANNE: He's lost consciousness, but he's still breathing. (two o'clock can be heard striking) Two o'clock! That's the hour foretold me. But to let him perish for want of aid. No. Let's take off his helmet. (going to a fountain near the chapel) A little water. He's coming to.

(Two or three Freebooters appear to the left, back. They point to Joan. Then leave to warn their companions.)

TALBOT: (coming to) Who has taken pity on me? These attentions? What do I see? Jeanne of Arc.

JEANNE: Drink and return to life with freedom.

TALBOT: You, my liberator. (shouts of fury from the left, Talbot rises) Ah, leave me, leave me. Your enemies. Don't you hear them?

JEANNE: (marching towards the gate after having retaken her banner) They won't dare to follow me into our walls. (Just as she reaches the drawbridge a cannon shot is heard. The drawbridge rises in front of her. She stops confused and says with defeat.) Delivered!

(Meanwhile English soldiers and Freebooters, headed by Robert and William, enter from all sides and surround Joan.)

ALL: It's she. It's Jeanne the sorceress.

WILLIAM: She's ours! We must take her alive. Who will dare to touch her?

ROBERT: Not I.

ALL: Nor I.

WILLIAM: Well! Let's all shoot at her together.

TALBOT: Stop. She's the one who just saved me.

SOME SOLDIERS: (lowering their weapons) The son of the General.

WILLIAM: (still aiming) She's also the one who saved

Orléans.

TALBOT: (rushing him and knocking down his weapon) Wretch! If she hadn't staunched my blood, protected my life, she would be safe with her own. No, no. Hell has no part in her work. I was her prisoner. She freed me. Let her be in her turn. (shouting toward the walls) Lower the drawbridge for the heroine of France. (silence) What? They don't answer me! Well, soldiers, make room for the noble girl who's fighting for her country. Honor to her whose feet we would kiss if she were English! Soldiers, open your ranks. (the soldiers begin to obey when Tyndal and his Freebooters appear)

TYNDAL: Freebooters! If she takes a step, death to the sorceress.

TALBOT: Tyndal—

TYNDAL: Yes, Tyndal. One single time he dropped his sword and it's this Devil's daughter who made his hand fall; also Tyndal swore to avenge himself for the death of his companions, the shame and dismay of the English.

TALBOT: I won't suffer it.

TYNDAL: My brave freebooters, surround the Captain— and us, for us, cry shame on her.

TALBOT: (surrounded) Cowardly bandit.

TYNDAL: (to his men who hesitate; Joan remains overwhelmed) You don't dare approach her, Well, as for me, I dare. (tearing the banner from her and hurling it to the ground) Down with the Devil's standard!

ROBERT: She's taken! The Captain's hand is not burned. She's only a girl.

GENERAL SHOUT: Glory to Tyndal!

DURAND: (running in from the left, eluding soldiers who try to stop him) No. It's not possible. I want to see her.

TYNDAL: (leading him near her) Here, look at her carefully, so as to go tell yours that her spells are broken, that the charm is shattered.

DURAND: (weeping at Joan's feet) Jeanne! My beloved Jeanne. What are they going to do to you?

JEANNE: Send me to God from whence I came. (falls to her knees)

ALL THE ENGLISH: (surrounding Joan who remains kneeling, shouting furiously) Glory to England! Glory to Tyndal! Victory for the Leopard. Death to Jeanne the Witch!

CURTAIN

ACT IV

Scene 7: The Judgment

The stage represents the cemetery of Saint Ouen. Tombs the length of the walls. In the back a hill covered with tombs and funerary monuments, and on which the people can be present at the judgment of Joan of Arc. In the background the Church of Saint Ouen which belongs to the cemetery. On each side of the stage a platform is raised hung in black. The one on the left, higher than the other, is intended for the judges. That on the right, reserved for Joan. To the right of the hill, the entry gate to the cemetery. Near the front of the stage, on the same side, is the guard box whose door opens near the platform on which Joan will be placed. D'Estivet and Tyndal enter through the cemetery gate.

TYNDAL: You think there's security enough here for you to listen to me?

D'ESTIVET: (dressed in black) Only here. As the Promoter of this trial I need to be extremely prudent. And I know your violence. I am listening to you.

TYNDAL: Then understand: my men and I are tired of so many delays. What! Today a whole year has gone by since this whore was captured. You needed six months to convince the Burgundians to deliver her to you. And since then you've held her in the tower of Rouen. You indict scribblings and interrogatories, and still you promised me to avenge the death of my brothers, surprised, slaughtered in the battle at Tournelles.

D'ESTIVET: All this is going to finish.

TYNDAL: We don't believe it; they're deceiving us.

D'ESTIVET: No. Everything's going to finish, I tell you. The Masters have bribed the Duke of Burgundy. She must die by judgment and torture. If she's not condemned as a sorceress, then she worked miracles, and Heaven is against the English.

TYNDAL: Well! Burn her right away.

D'ESTIVET: The Doctors say that the Devil cannot have commerce with a pure young virgin.

TYNDAL: Well, it's likely the Devil will soon want her. Yes, she's got to die. For the life of this woman is a shame and a torment to me. If her death has been resolved, what's the use of bringing her here?

D'ESTIVET: Up till now she's always been questioned behind closed doors and by those I chose. These questions with some suppressions and some additions have been sent to the University of Paris. To the Clergy of Rouen. We have their reply which is all we need. But the trial must have a certain appearance of openness.

TYNDAL: So be it! I leave you to do all your jabbering today. But think carefully, that I and my Freebooters will be here. They are not always led as one wishes. Think that I hate this girl because she vanquished us; because she defeated me. I hate her for her glory; for her reputation for virtue, for her beauty. To trample all that underfoot. Oh, that will be my joy. And my triumph. Do this today, still; but then let us act! She's going to come. I am going to place myself on her passage and I won't lose sight of her. (he leaves, D'Estivet's clerk enters)

CLERK: Milord, the judges are assembled at Saint Ouen and are awaiting you.

D'ESTIVET: I am going to meet them. (they leave)

TALBOT: (appearing at the left, supporting a woman whose head is covered with a hood, leading her to the guard box at the right) Courage. But in the name of Heaven, don't budge. By half opening the door you can see and hear her.

(The cemetery gate opens. Guards enter first, then the

people, then the freebooters headed by Tyndal. They spread around the back of the stage to the edge of the hill. Then comes d'Estivet and the Judges, who go to the platform on the left. New guards bring in Joan who stops before the tribunal, Joan is dressed as in Scene II.)

JEANNE: Milord Promoter, passing before the Church of Saint Ouen I asked to make my prayer there. It's such a long time since I prayed in a church. The beadle, Massieu, refused to let me.

D'ESTIVET: The beadle only acted on my orders. You cannot enter a church in the dress of a man. If you are a good Christian, all places must be good for you to pray. Go!

(The guards point to Joan the scaffold on the right. Joan takes a few steps then kneels.)

JEANNE: My God! It's a year today since I fought for the last time. Since that time, through many sorrows and vexations you've brought me to this final ordeal. Since that time I have no news of the King, the leaders, all those of the time of my mission. All those of the regretted days of my childhood have doubtless been unable to come to me. I am indeed alone. Lord, support to the end, the servant who has obeyed you.

D'ESTIVET: Lead the accused to her place. (the clerk leads her to the platform on the right where she is placed between two beadles) Jeanne, a sincere repentance and a confession of your spells could disarm your judges. Answer. Have you heard voices again?

JEANNE: Yes, last night.

D'ESTIVET: What did they say to you?

JEANNE: To reply to you without fear.

D'ESTIVET: Jeanne, by means of what sorcery do you lead your soldiers to victory?

JEANNE: The soldiers! I said to them: March boldly! And I marched first.

D'ESTIVET: Why was your standard borne higher in the Church of Rheims than those of the other captains?

JEANNE: It was difficult. It was indeed right for it to be honored.

D'ESTIVET: Do you persist in believing that you have not committed a crime, an outrage of religion by wearing this male attire?

JEANNE: No. And again at this time, if I were with our people, and in this attire, it seems that would be one of the great virtues of France, to do what I was doing before I was captured.

D'ESTIVET: So you persist in your hate against the English?

JEANNE: I persist in my love for my country.

D'ESTIVET: And if you could escape from this prison?

JEANNE: I would do it at the risk of my life. Hasn't it been said: Help yourself, Heaven will help you?

D'ESTIVET: And you would again take up arms?

JEANNE: Why are you tempting me with these words? My task is fulfilled and I no longer must fight. But I know quite well that without me the foreigners will all be thrown out of France, excepting—

D'ESTIVET: Excepting?

JEANNE: Excepting those who will die here. (murmuring among the people and the freebooters)

D'ESTIVET: Then you believe that God does not love the English?

JEANNE: In England, he loves them. Not in France. (renewed murmurs) Oh, I know quite well the English will make me die. Thinking, after my death to regain the kingdom of France. But be they 100,000 times more than they are now, they will never have this kingdom.

FREEBOOTERS and A GROUP OF THE PEOPLE:

Death! Death to the sorceress!

TALBOT: (placing himself in the middle of the stage) Judges, be respectful of the accused. When you allow these furiously blinded men to intervene in the trial by means of their shouts and their threats, it's time that a voice be raised for her.

D'ESTIVET: You do not have the right to speak.

TALBOT: Then I take it! I take it in the name of my father, your supporter, the savior of all. I take it in the name of England to spare England a crime, an eternal dishonor! Jeanne fought, she was victorious, and to punish her for it, to console the pride of those she beat, you are making a hypocritical trial for her. You accuse her of witchcraft! You chain her in a dungeon. At night you place near her soldiers who insult her, who outrage her, who at every moment wake her to say, "Jeanne, tomorrow's the day you will burn." In the name of all! in the name of Heaven: Justice!

TYNDAL and THE FREEBOOTERS: Vengeance! Vengeance!

D'ESTIVET: Yes, vengeance in the name of your King, Milord William Talbot. Vengeance in the name of Heaven! A terrible punishment for she who fought you through the power of Hell!

ALL: Hell!

D'ESTIVET: Yes, I can bring to the tribunal a proof, a witness that she won't dare challenge.

ALL: Listen! Listen!

D'ESTIVET: Well, chance led me to Domremy the very day you left, Jeanne. And I was present at the goodbyes with your family. Your father withdrew from you in terror, and defeated by the evidence he caused the word "sorcery" to be heard.

ALL: Sorcery!

D'ESTIVET: Yes, Jeanne. It's your father himself who accuses you. Recently again, charged with investigating your trial, I returned to this village; I saw this unfortunate old man again. I saw him again on his death bed.

JEANNE: What have you said? O Heaven!

D'ESTIVET: And this word that condemns you he repeated again in his last moments, and he went back to God after having signed this writing.

JEANNE: (in despair) My father! Dead!

JUDGES: Read!

PEOPLE: Listen! Listen!

D'ESTIVET: (reading) "I commend my poor daughter to

the clemency of her judges. Her heart was good and pure. She willed the good and if she has done ill, it was not by her, it was the work of the demon."

(At these words, a great scream by a woman can be heard. Everyone looks to the right.)

JEANNE: (with emotion) That shout—

D'ESTIVET: What's it mean?

(The woman Talbot brought in comes to cast herself on her knees before the tribunal.)

ISABELLE: Ah, hear, hear me, Milords!

D'ESTIVET: But who is this woman?

ISABELLE: (raising her hood) Isabelle d'Arc.

JEANNE: My mother.

ALL: Her mother!

(All sorts of reactions. Joan weeping, extends her arms to her mother.)

D'ESTIVET: Withdraw! We cannot hear you.

DIFFERING VOICES: Yes! Yes! No! No!

TALBOT: Refuse to hear a mother when you accuse her child! That's impossible! She will speak, I wish it, I demand it. It's I who led her here to you, Milords; I who have taken her under my protection. Because she has the right to defend and repulse slander.

ISABELLE: (forcefully) Yes, slander. Her father! Him, curse her, accuse her after he had learned to know her better? Ah, if you had seen him during his last days, as he wept, thinking of her. "Pardon" he said, "Pardon your father who understands and admires you now. Jeanne, don't let me die without having pardoned me." (pointing to d'Estivet) It was then this man appeared in the doorway of our hut. He approached him. "They wish to condemn your daughter," he said, "and you alone can save her by asking mercy of her judges. Here! This paper, it's her salvation. It's your daughter's life." He signed. Could he think that to kill the child they would use the hand of her father! Then he died in my arms, repeating, "My daughter, my poor Jeanne, pardon me, pardon me." Oh, this time one cannot be deceived by the voice of a mother, and it's by her, by my child, that I swear. Yes, may Heaven strike her this instant if I am not speaking the truth.

TALBOT: (addressing the judges) You cannot condemn her, Milords. That would make you accomplices in such perfidy! It's impossible!

SEVERAL JUDGES and A GROUP OF THE PEOPLE: Yes, yes, impossible.

TYNDAL: Do you hear? The tribunal is sold.

FREEBOOTERS: Enough, judges. Death to the judges!

A SECTION OF THE PEOPLE: Jeanne is innocent. Let her live. Justice! Justice!

(General uproar. The Freebooters, coming down from the hill despite the people, and the guards are ready to invade the tribunal.)

D'ESTIVET: (rising, dominating the tumult) Guards, protect the tribunal and execute the orders you've received. (the guards succeed in pressing back the crowd as d'Estivet consults the judges surrounding him, then dictates to his clerk near him) The tribunal has pronounced. (the tumult subsides, but the Freebooters have moved forward and the remainder of the populace, pushed back by them, now occupy the hill at the back)

D'ESTIVET: Jeanne, rise. Your crimes are proven. And yet the tribunal still wants to give proof to you of an excess of clemency. Sign this writing instantly, by which you declare forever to renounce these clothes which you ought never to have worn.

(The clerk approaches. Joan hesitates. Talbot and Isabelle supplicate her.)

JEANNE: (to clerk) Guide my hand. I cannot write. A cross! (She remits the paper after having made a cross.

The clerk delivers it to the hands of d'Estivet.)

D'ESTIVET: (in a strong, solemn voice) In the name of Henry VI, King of England and France, the Judges order that Jeanne of Arc, of Domremy, return to her prison, there to weep for her sins until her last hour. And if she ever forgets the promise she has just made in the presence of this tribunal she will be instantly led to the stake. (new rumors of various sorts) Captain Tyndal, to you the protection of the prisoner.

TYNDAL: (coming center stage) Mine! At last!

D'ESTIVET: (aside) Those clothes. It will indeed be necessary that she resume them. (making a sign to take Joan away)

(Tyndal and his men lead Joan towards the gate of the cemetery. Talbot goes to Isabelle.)

ISABELLE: (falling to her knees) O my god! You've performed so many miracles for her. Won't you do one to return her to her mother?

CURTAIN

ACT V

Scene 8: The Prison of Rouen

The stage represents the interior of a prison. In the back an alcove raised on two or three steps and closed by a rough curtain. To the right, at an angle, the entrance door. Also at the right, a table and two stools. William and Robert are playing dice. The stage is weakly lit by a single light placed on the table.

WILLIAM: (throwing the dice) Six.

ROBERT: (throwing in his turn) Seven. You lost.

WILLIAM: That's fair. Up to me to do it. (going cautiously towards the alcove, half opening the curtain at the foot of the bed, he puts several items together which he places in a package; then, going to the window at the left, he tosses the package through the window. Robert, chin in hand, watches him do it. William resumes his place at the table.)

WILLIAM: (sitting down) My revenge.

ROBERT: That's agreed.

WILLIAM: (tossing the dice) Five!

ROBERT: (tossing) Four.

WILLIAM: Now, your turn.

ROBERT: So be it. (taking the clothes Joan wore, in the second and seventh scenes, from a chair placed near the table, he opens the curtain of the alcove by the corner and places the clothes in the alcove. William observes him, chin in hand.)

WILLIAM: That's not all. Since you lost the last round, it's still up to you to take the flask.

ROBERT: What's that?

WILLIAM: To pour that liquor in the cup which is there by the bed where that young girl is sleeping.

ROBERT: No. This is getting serious.

WILLIAM: Huh?

ROBERT: I've never poisoned.

WILLIAM: I repeat to you it's not a question of poisoning, but only of procuring for her a calm, deep sleep lasting several hours.

ROBERT: And we will leave?

WILLIAM: As soon as the Captain comes to tell us we can go.

ROBERT: Tyndal; alone near Jeanne, sleeping!

WILLIAM: What's it to you? Take that flask.

ROBERT: No, no! I tell you I don't dare.

WILLIAM: Imbecile! As if what we did wasn't really much more dangerous for her.

ROBERT: You. You only took her woman's clothes from her. And you threw them in the courtyard of the prison.

WILLIAM: And you?

ROBERT: As for me, I put in their place her male attire. I don't see great harm in that.

WILLIAM: Truly? Then you are forgetting that Jeanne, under penalty of being burned, signed a pledge never to wear the clothes of a man.

ROBERT: At her waking, she will be free to do as she wishes.

WILLIAM: At her waking? Didn't they order us to be present at her waking?

ROBERT: Yes, all. And glass in hand.

WILLIAM: Well?

ROBERT: Well, I get it, When she opens her eyes in the midst of her shouts of joy and drunkenness she's going to recoil in shock and resume this outfit. The only one we've left in her cell.

WILLIAM: That's the very thing. Those who want to destroy her, lacking the skin of the wolf, sew on that of the fox.

ROBERT: All this is the work of the Promoter, the Sire D'Estivet. You, me, the comrades, the Captain himself: we are only his instruments. It's he who oversees, who directs everything in this prison.

WILLIAM: Keep it down. Perhaps he hears us at this moment.

ROBERT: That's true. And you want me to accomplish the will of that man. (points to flask)

WILLIAM: I intend that together we earn our 300 gold shillings.

ROBERT: 300!

WILLIAM: There's the wherewithal for you to retire; you, who say you've had enough of this job.

ROBERT: Well— But why don't you do it yourself?

WILLIAM: Chance designated you. Take it and proceed.

ROBERT: You're really sure she's asleep?

WILLIAM: Eh! Yes. Since just now she neither saw nor heard us. Well! You aren't going to proceed?

ROBERT: This is like I was stealing on an altar?

WILLIAM: Hurry up! It seems to me that I heard the door of the tower opening overhead. It's probably the Captain.

ROBERT: Approach with me. (They both go forward hesitatingly. William draws the curtain. Joan is revealed, sleeping on a mat covered with an old linen rug.) That's not the face of a witch! (goes to pour the contents of the flask into the cup, then stops) Her lips are moving.

WILLIAM: (pushing him) Eh, no.

JEANNE: (in her sleep) Jesus protect me.

ROBERT: (recoiling in horror and letting the flask fall) I don't want it! I don't want it!

WILLIAM: (looking at the broken flask) You spilled it. (lets the curtain fall)

ROBERT: So much the better. It's a judgment of Heaven.

WILLIAM: The Devil's in it.

ROBERT: (noticing Tyndal who enters) The Captain.

WILLIAM: Shut up. We won't get anything.

TYNDAL: My orders?

WILLIAM: (stepping in front of Robert who is shaking) Executed, Captain.

TYNDAL: (tossing him a purse) Fine. Leave me. (William heads towards the door, Robert doesn't dare budge) Why aren't you leaving?

ROBERT: (recovering from his terror and leaving precipitously) I'm going, Captain, I'm going. (they leave)

TYNDAL: (alone) There she is! The English have delivered her to me. No human obstacle. She's mine! Her voice, even her look, enchained in sleep. Jeanne, you disdained Tiphaine, the peasant. You covered him with shame. And now, here you are in his power. (Going to the alcove and violently opening the curtain. Joan wakes up and half rises. Tyndal recoils.) Ah!

JEANNE: (rising in terror, dressed in light sleeping clothes) Are you the executioner? Is it death you are bringing me?

TYNDAL: No. They took away your arms, your banner, your invincible arms and your inspired name. A last prestige remains to you.

JEANNE: Oh. Kill me! Kill me!

TYNDAL: No. They'd call you martyr, they'd call you saint. (Joan tries vainly to shake the door) Oh, these walls won't open before you.

JEANNE: Great God!

TYNDAL: Your voice won't be heard. Or rather, to your shouts of despair they are going to reply with insults. Around this prison there are only soldiers who obey me blindly, or men devoted to the Promoter. From your ruin, he expects the triumph of his ambition and favors from England. As for me, I expect my vengeance! Jeanne, you've surrounded yourself with a prestige of purity which imposes on men; elevated you to a hellish power. You won't leave here except to serve as the laughingstock of men and demons. And even the power of that God which protects you won't save you.

JEANNE: (on her knees) Ah! pity! pity! It's a horrible crime, an infamous perfidy by my enemies! Why, as for me, I fought in broad daylight; I fought only for my country to be free, for our mothers to be respected. They could kill me in battle, although I've never killed. And they condemned me to live on, to grow old in a circle of stone. Pity for me! pity. Doubtless you have a wife, a daughter?

TYNDAL: I have neither wife nor daughter.

JEANNE: (still on her knees) But you can listen to prayer. You can let yourself be appeased. You don't want to become an object of horror.

TYNDAL: (raising her violently) I intend to have my revenge. (He advances toward Joan who retreats to the table with the light. Tyndal's face is lit up.)

JEANNE: Tiphaine! I recognize you.

TYNDAL: (momentarily confused) Me! Me!

JEANNE: Oh, it's you! You! French. You from Lorraine, you from Domremy.

TYNDAL: Well, yes, it's me. Who to obtain revenge for your disdain left my country, abandoned my ancient mother, lived for pillage and blood. See how I must hate you. And to my hate, measure my joy in seeing you there, shivering under my glance, quaking under my hand.

JEANNE: (suddenly jerking free with sublime energy) On

your knees, wretch! Your mother is watching you.

TYNDAL: My mother!

JEANNE: Your mother! dead.

TYNDAL: Dead. My mother! dead!

JEANNE: In my arms!

TYNDAL: In your arms!

JEANNE: Your mother cursed the traitor to his country. The traitor to his brothers.

TYNDAL: No, no.

JEANNE: She cursed him under his terrifying surname.

TYNDAL: She didn't know.

JEANNE: Malediction on the renegade, the most infamous of all English executioners. Vile assassin of honor, who came at night, during sleep. surprising the one from whom they've taken forever, the air, the sun, the sight of the world, freedom. To steal from her, her only possession: her purity, her honor, her consolation, her eternal glory. Oh, the cowardly accursed.

TYNDAL: Oh, no, no. I don't want to be coward. I don't want to be cursed!

JEANNE: Ask pardon of France.

TYNDAL: Yes, I betrayed her.

JEANNE: Of your brothers.

TYNDAL: Yes, I've spilled their blood.

JEANNE: Of Heaven!

TYNDAL: Yes, I've disregarded its power which sent a messenger of its will. Yes, I've meditated against you a nocturnal attack and outrage. I've done more. Outraged, ruined, I wanted to deliver you to scorn, to the laughter of the wretches I command. Before daybreak they will be here, invited by me to the spectacle of your shame. To you, Jeanne, who harvested the last sigh of my mother, to you, daughter of Heaven— Pardon! Pardon!

JEANNE: (exalted) My God! Unarmed and prisoner, you've again made me conqueror. For you and for France. Pardon him and don't curse him.

TYNDAL: Jeanne, for that prayer, my life, my blood.

SHOUTS: (outside) Tyndal! Tyndal!

JEANNE: What's that noise?

TYNDAL: (worried) I shiver. And yet it's not time.

JEANNE: Answer.

TYNDAL: My soldiers!

JEANNE: Your soldiers.

TYNDAL: Drunk and coming to insult the broken virgin.

JEANNE: Ah, Great God. Who will stop them?

TYNDAL: I will.

JEANNE: Yes, a moment, just one. So that at least I don't have to submit to the outrage of their glances.

TYNDAL: I will watch over you, and in defending you, I will regain the right to fight and die for my country.

JEANNE: Thanks! Thanks! Child of France. (rushing behind the curtain and shutting it)

TYNDAL: (momentarily alone) Child of France. Ah, that name. I again feel myself worthy of bearing it. (shouts of the Freebooters grow closer) It's them. Let them come. I am watching over her.

(The Freebooters rush on stage, cups in hand.)

FREEBOOTERS: Long live Tyndal! Glory to Tyndal!

ROBERT: To the Captain!

ALL: To the Captain!

WILLIAM: To the Virgin of Domremy.

ALL: To the Virgin of Domremy!

WILLIAM: And Jeanne, Jeanne. Where is she?

ALL: Where is she? We want to see her. We need her! Jeanne! Jeanne!

TYNDAL: (placing himself before the curtains and drawing his sword) The first of you to come forward, I mean to kill at my feet.

(Astonishment)

WILLIAM: Heavens! The Captain is jealous. (laughter)

ROBERT: Has she enchanted him, too?

ALL: The Magician! The Magician. Where is she?

(They advance. The curtain opens and Joan appears in men's apparel. At the same moment d'Estivet comes through the door with his guards.)

JEANNE: Get back, wretches, get back.

D'ESTIVET: (coming mid-stage as the Freebooters recoil before Joan) By the terms of the Judgment of the Cemetery of Saint Ouen, Jeanne of Arc, of Domremy, having resumed the apparel of a man, despite her promise, is declared to have relapsed; a heretic and, as such, will be delivered to the secular arm to undergo the punishment of fire.

JEANNE: (defeated) Mother, I will never see you again.

TYNDAL: I will save you or die in front of you.

(The guards surround Joan. The Curtain Falls.)

CURTAIN

ACT V

Scene 9: The Stake

The square of the Old Market in Rouen. On the left, near the spectators, the town hall. Opposite this, a stone bench. In the back, a huge pyre on the top of which is a stake to which the victim is attached.

AT RISE, guards garrison the entrances and prevent the people from approaching.

TYNDAL: (entering from the left) He's not coming. Well, I've vainly counted on him. Or rather, has he been killed trying to obey me? Ah, there he is.

ROBERT: (entering from the right) Captain!

TYNDAL: It's you, Robert. You really had to wait?

ROBERT: It's because of the tumult and disorder. En- cumbered by all the streets of the town it was difficult for me to join the comrades.

TYNDAL: At last.

ROBERT: I saw them.

TYNDAL: And you promised them?

ROBERT: All that you told me to tell them, I said, Captain.

TYNDAL: And I will keep my word to them, to you. All the riches that sacking and pillaging have brought me. But they must obey me. Obey me to save Jeanne, as blindly as you did to assure her ruin.

ROBERT: I am with you.

TYNDAL: But your companions?

ROBERT: They will do like me.

TYNDAL: An hour remains to us.

ROBERT: No, Captain. They suspected an action in her favor and the moment of execution has been advanced.

TYNDAL: What are you saying?

ROBERT: The escort is already en route.

TYNDAL: Well— You will follow me there. We will stir up the people on our way. And we will still arrive to de-

stroy the pyre and free the victim. Come, I want to re-
pair, by this last action, all the crimes of my life. Come,
Robert, come.

(They exit extreme left. From the opposite side d'Estivet
and an officer enter.)

D'ESTIVET: (to officer) Push back the people. Where is
the Duke of Bedford?

OFFICER: At the town hall.

D'ESTIVET: Vainly they riot, conspire, take up arms to
tear the prisoner from us. Everything has been foreseen
and the vengeance of England is certain. (Goes into the
town hall. At the back, noise of the crowd at the head of
the procession.)

SHOUTS OF THE PEOPLE: There she is! There she is!

(Joan enters with the procession. After some murmurs
there is a profound silence. Durand is at the right of the
crowd, ready, despite the soldiers to rush to her, From the
left, Talbot appears approaching.)

JEANNE: (offering her hand to Durand who kisses it re-
gretfully) You, Durand! I am not alone to suffer my
martyrdom.

DURAND: To admire and bless you, all the people, our
brothers, are here.

TALBOT: And among the English, more than one refuses to be associated with England's crime.

JEANNE: Talbot.

TALBOT: Yes, Talbot, protected, saved by you, and whose voice has been powerless to save you. I asked if I was permitted to exchange your ransom against that of my father, now a French prisoner. They refused. I offered all my wealth as the price of your liberty. They refused again, telling me, that in accordance with our treaties, The King of France, himself alone, had the right to repurchase Jeanne of Arc.

JEANNE: The King. When I am dying for him, does he think of me at all?

TALBOT: Perhaps! And if my hope is not deceived, if she's been able to reach him—

JEANNE: She—who's that?

VOICE: (off) Jeanne! Jeanne!

TALBOT: Listen! That voice. Do you recognize it?

(Isabelle enters from the back fighting her way through the guards.)

ISABELLE: Jeanne! Jeanne!

JEANNE: My mother!

ISABELLE: (breathless) Her safety. Her deliverance! (she waves a parchment)

JEANNE: (supporting her) My good mother. (they make her sit on the stone bench)

PEOPLE: Saved! They're going to save her.

ISABELLE: I can do no more.

JEANNE: (supporting her) My good mother.

TALBOT: (taking the parchment) The Royal Seal of France. To the Governor of Rouen. I understand. There! There! (to the guards) Suspend the punishment. I, Talbot, order it. You see the Royal Seal. It's Jeanne's safety. I am running to find the Duke of Bedford. Until my return, respect this young girl. And you, Jeanne, hope! hope!

JEANNE: (looking at her mother) She's coming to!

DURAND: My God! What's wrong with her?

ISABELLE: Jeanne. Durand. Ah, I want to pray. To thank God and I am only able to weep.

JEANNE: You wanted to see me again.

ISABELLE: I wanted to take you back again, to take you with me to the country, to hide you in my arms, and to live very old to love you longer. (with spirit) My God. How happy I am.

SAINTRAILLES: In the name of Heaven! What has happened?

DURAND: Speak quickly, aunt Isabelle.

ISABELLE: When they condemned you in the cemetery of Saint Ouen, the worthy English lord who was there—

JEANNE: Talbot.

ISABELLE: He told me that they would watch over you and that he himself could not guide my steps but that one of his faithful servants would take me and escort me to the King of France.

JEANNE: What are you saying? To the King—

ISABELLE: I found him. They didn't want to let me go to him. I braved all. I threw myself at his feet. "I cannot," he said. He was talking about his treasure. I didn't listen to a thing. "It's needed for my daughter. She's being destroyed for you. You must to do it for her." I retained him. I wouldn't leave his hands. Finally, vanquished, he said to me, "Let me write." And this letter, your freedom, your life, I brought it. (frightened) Where is it?

DURAND: Lord Talbot took it to the governor.

JEANNE: (allowing herself to soften) God and dear mother.

ISABELLE: Jeanne! Jeanne, my beloved!

DURAND: (pointing to the guards and the people) Don't let them see our joy. They are all looking at us uneasily.

(The remainder is in lowered voices)

ISABELLE: (to Joan) You were not weeping just now; and—now—

JEANNE: Now, I can admit that to die at nineteen is very young. To leave everything, without seeing one's mother again, one's friends, one's country, the land of one's father. (with terror) Then this stake. It's a terrible torture. (hiding in the breast of her mother) Oh, I was afraid! I was afraid.

TALBOT: (returning) The Duke of Bedford holds in his hand the message of Charles VII. England will not be soiled by a sacrilegious murder.

ISABELLE: Don't weep anymore, my child. Raise your head. Look at Heaven. It's a beautiful day in May. Every year on the Thirtieth of May you will thank God for having saved France; I will thank the Virgin for having saved my daughter.

D'ESTIVET: (entering from the town hall, to his guards) Let justice be done.

SAINTRAILLES: What did you say? O Heaven. And yet, this letter from the King of France.—

D'ESTIVET: The King of France asks for a delay of a few days to send the ransom of Jeanne of Arc. England doesn't choose to wait!

(Screams by Isabelle and those around her.)

D'ESTIVET: (to the executioner) Do your duty.

ISABELLE: Ah, it's impossible! My daughter. The King told me—

DURAND: The King? Are we still reduced to this? My God! What! The King doesn't have in his treasury the wherewithal to save her life?

ISABELLE: Of the one who saved his crown.

SAINTRAILLES: (aside) The King. Yesterday, again, he gave a feast for Madame Agnes.

ISABELLE: And you are going to perish for the one who is forgetting you.

JEANNE: Not for him alone, mother. For the people. They will never forget me.

D'ESTIVET: (to the men of justice) Obey!

ISABELLE: Oh! I conjure you! My daughter! My daughter!

JEANNE: (kissing her hand) Heaven spare her the sorrow of my last goodbye. Durand, my friend, my brother, you will watch over her, and then you tell the people how much I love them and that my last thought was of them. (to d'Estivet) Promoter of the trial, I die by you. But I pardon you. May God forgive you. Lord, in saving my country, I thought to obey you. If I've sinned, have pity on me. The France for whom I die, complete her deliverance. And if you are punishing her by a foreign invasion let my memory have the power for her deliverance, that you loaned me during my life. You all, my friends, my enemies, while I go to suffer my last sorrow, pray for my soul and ask that this evening my soul be in paradise. (turning, she sees her banner that an English officer has just brought in at a command of d'Estivet) My banner!

D'ESTIVET: (giving it to her) Condemned to be burned—like you.

JEANNE: Give me, give me! And this time, I thank you, England! (taking her banner and clutching it with enthusiasm) Yes, we must end together. It's with you I will carry off my last victory. (The penitents fall to their knees. With resolution she mounts to the stake to which the executioner attaches her. He starts the fire.) Climb down quickly, the fire will reach you.

(Outside, shots can be heard. Tyndal enters running, staggering, sword in hand, wounded. He falls near the stake then rises on his knees before Joan.)

TYNDAL: Jeanne, they've killed me because I wanted to protect you. Ah, like you, perhaps, my mother will pardon me.

JEANNE: (with enthusiasm, while celestial music is now heard) Yes, my voices were from God. Yes, my voices did not deceive me. (The flames reach her. Her head falls and she screams.) Jesus! (she dies)

TYNDAL: (rising with a final effort) English! You've just killed a Saint.

TALBOT: A saint, according to God.

DURAND: A Saint, according to the Nation!

(Tyndal falls at the foot of the pyre. Thunder growls, lightning flashes, and all fall to their knees.)

CURTAIN

ACT V

Scene 10: Apotheosis

Clouds have enveloped the pyre. Little by little they disappear. On the site of the pyre one sees a sort of luminous car in which the Archangel appears beside Joan. In the back, the celestial abode of the elect. Then the clouds develop during the following verses spoken by the Archangel

ARCHANGEL:
Rush Jeanne,
Toward your brothers in paradise.
And to console you in your sufferings
That the accursed reduced you to,
Behold the destinies predicted
For your brothers in France.
Your martyrdom is fertile
And your blood's just opened
A new era to the French.
It knows how it must suffer for it
How it must die.—

The centuries march on;—courage, honor
Are going to complete the work of independence
For from your pyre begins
The march of a great people
To glory, to happiness.

(The clouds swirl and one sees in turn tableaus of the taking of the Bastille, then the day of the Bridge of Arible in 1830. The orchestra plays alternatively airs from the Marseilles and the Parisienne.)

ARCHANGEL:
Plunge your eyes into the infinite sphere.
Of happier days the future is endowed.
For by the genius of France
Is promised to humanity.
Already, everything concurs and
Is going well
To better ascend the powerful harmony
Of order and liberty.

(The clouds which have, bit by bit, enveloped the stage reopen again. In the back one sees a fantastic palace in which the genius of arts, wearing a luminous halo, completes sculpting a statue of Joan of Arc.)

ARCHANGEL:
Then offering the people
A legitimate homage,
The God of Arts will retrace the image
Of your proud and chaste beauty.

To attach renown to its meaning,
The artist demands for your glory
A ray of immortality.

CURTAIN

ABOUT FRANK J. MORLOCK

FRANK J. MORLOCK has written and translated many plays since retiring from the legal profession in 1992. His translations have also appeared on Project Gutenberg, the Alexandre Dumas Père web page, Literature in the Age of Napoléon, Infinite Artistries.com, and Munsey's (formerly Blackmask). In 2006 he received an award from the North American Jules Verne Society for his translations of Verne's plays. He lives and works in México.

www.ingramcontent.com/pod-product-compliance
Lightning Source LLC
Chambersburg PA
CBHW032002040426
42448CB00006B/455